Praise for
Workplace Spirituality: A Complete Guide for Business Leaders

Smith shows us a way to spirituality that is well-integrated into our overall lives and tolerant of differing beliefs, but that still holds each of us accountable to our gods and each other. Her kinder, gentler, and inclusive approach is a welcome antidote to the angry religiosity we see too often in the headlines.

> —Robert D. Austin, Harvard Business School professor and co-author of
> *Artful Making: What Managers Need to Know About How Artists Work*

Nancy Smith's thoroughly researched exploration of workplace spirituality draws on sources as diverse as ancient folktales from around the world, books by leading economic experts, and popular news media. It's particularly gratifying that she devotes several chapters to ethics and social responsibility—and that the book not only affirms Smith's own Christian faith but is careful to validate other religious traditions as well.

> —Shel Horowitz, author of *Principled Profit: Marketing That Puts People First*
> and founder of the Business Ethics Pledge

Workplace Spirituality is an insightful and comprehensive presentation of an important new focus on spiritual presence. Smith's up-to-date coverage of recent writings gives the reader a comprehensive intro-duction to important writings in the field. Her wholistic understanding of what the spiritual is means that she not only covers relating at work to the Mystery which is at the center of life, but she also addresses our corresponding response to that encounter in our ethical relationships
both in the workplace and in the national and global relationships that are affected by the workplace.

> —Stephen Charles Mott, author of *A Christian Perspective on Political Thought* and *Biblical Ethics and Social Change;* Retired pastor and former Professor of Christian Social Ethics, Gordon-Conwell Theological Seminary

This is the book on spirituality in the workplace we've all been waiting for; short, to the point, and eminently practical. Nancy Smith has been a significant contributor to the spirit at work community for a long time, and this book will inform, inspire, and guide you to effectively integrate your spiritual values with work that is meaningful and rewarding.

> —Judi Neal, Ph.D., Executive Director, Association for Spirit at Work;
> Founder, International Spirit at Work Awards;
> President, Neal & Associates

About the Author

 Nancy Smith has 20 years' experience as a technical writer, supervisor, and manager in high tech software companies. She also has more than 15 years in Christian ministry as an educator, course designer, retreat leader, spiritual director, and coach.

An ordained United Methodist Deacon, Smith has her M.Div. from Boston University and is a graduate of the Guild for Spiritual Guidance. Currently enrolled in a post-graduate program in the Practice of Spirituality (Spiritual Direction) at Boston College, Smith's passion is to help people and workplaces become open to the gifts of all spiritualities at work.

Smith's knowledge and expertise in the area of Workplace Spirit-uality are recognized in the media. She has been a guest on *The Business Shrink* talk show and has been quoted in several publications, including *Sales and Marketing Management* and *Interpreter* mag-azines. Smith maintains a website that she began five years ago at http://www.WorkplaceSpirituality.info, from which she sends out a monthly e-newsletter.

Nancy Smith lives in Peabody, Massachusetts with her husband Bob. They have two adult sons and four grandchildren.

Workplace Spirituality:

Complete

A ^ Guide for Business Leaders

By Nancy R. Smith

Axial Age Publishing
Peabody, Massachusetts

To my grandchildren Laura Elizabeth, Patrick David, Hanisi Hevani, and Hefrạni Maoaʻnoa, whose innocence and energy kept me grounded during the writing of this book. Blessings to you!

Cover design by Zoltan Rac-Sabo, www.the-it-factor.com

If you are unable to order this book from your local bookseller, you may order directly from the publisher. **Attention corporations and retreat centers:** For information on using our books as fundraisers, premiums, or gifts, contact the publisher:

P.O. Box 4246, Peabody, Massachusetts 01961
154C Shore Drive, Peabody, Massachusetts 01960
Phone: (978) 977-7785
Email: publicist@AxialAgePublishing.com
   www.AxialAgePublishing.com

Note: Some of the quoted materials are from authors around the world whose English spellings are different from those in the U.S. Such spellings are correct and have been preserved to respect the original writers as well as our global audience.

Categories:
Business & Economics/Management
Religion/Spirituality

ISBN: 0-9778047-3-9
FIRST EDITION
10 9 8 7 6 5 4 3 2 1
Printed in the United States of America

Acknowledgments

For those unique and especially skilled people who have provided their professional help in many ways during the writing of this book—you are indeed a Gift to me!

Ann R. Leach, my professional editor and a friend of many years, questioned my assumptions, suggested needed reorganizations, nagged me for all the grammatical and format details I either didn't know or forgot, kept her patience and diplomacy when I changed styles out of the boredom of looking at the text the same way all the time, verified many of the endnotes, and created the index. Without her, this book would be a chaotic mess. Those things that remain that detract from editorial orderliness can be attributed to my own errors or stubbornness.

Stephen C. Mott, long-time friend and mentor, was my careful reader, patiently challenging my assumptions and conclusions while encouraging me free to maintain my own voice, and shared his expertise on economics, ethics, and faith.

Zoltan Rac-Sabo of www.the-it-factor.com, a professional artist and designer patiently offered iterations of the book cover until his rendition took my breath away.

And as always, gratitude to my supportive family and friends, who have never stopped loving or encouraging me.

Contents

Introduction

ARE YOU AMONG THE. . .

72% of Americans *who work more than 40 hours per week?*

61% *who consider themselves overworked?*

86% *who are not satisfied with their job?*

82% *who are unhappy with their work/life balance?*

89% *of workers who hope to change jobs in the next six months?*

84% *who say the economy has hindered their ability to change jobs?*[1]

Are You an Over-Worked, Disillusioned Worker?

Workers are disillusioned with the scandals in business ethics, distrusting of employers and disappointed in corporate failures to live up to pension promises.

Sometimes the economy makes it necessary to "hunker down" and keep quiet about demands. But as they have come to recognize the end of job security, workers are also learning to take their careers into their own hands. And as they have learned to manage their own careers, they have also decided to look for a different kind of workplace:

> If I'm going to work for you, I want a decent salary—but I want more! I want you to conduct business ethically. I want you to

institute business practices that will preserve the environment for generations to come. I want you to see me as a person, not merely a 'resource.'

And I want a spiritually-friendly workplace where I can bring my whole self, be true to my own values, and make a satisfying contribution to the business.

Are you one of these workers? Or are you an employer who must deal with dissatisfied and demanding workers like these?

What Will You Find Here?

In this book, which is the first in a series of titles related to *Workplace Spirituality*, you will:

- Discover the origins and significance of the Workplace Spirituality movement and learn how it can benefit you as a worker, a leader, or a manager.

- Discover the seven essential traits of a spiritual person and the job-related behaviors that result from those traits.

- Consider the underlying economic theories and issues involved in business ethics and corporate social responsibility.

- Discover six principles for a spiritual workplace.

- Learn the differences between managers and leaders and the contributions both make to business.

- Reflect on six human issues that will help you become a spiritual leader.

- Consider six factors that are involved in changing cultural values in your workplace.

How Is this Book Organized?

This first title in the *Workplace Spirituality* series consists of four parts:

Part I: Why Workplace Spirituality and Why Now?

Part I consists of three chapters. It begins with definitions that clarify the difference between spirituality and religion, provides an overview of the workplace spirituality movement, and discusses our concepts of work itself:

1. What IS Workplace Spirituality?

2. Highlights of the Movement

3. The Purpose of Work in Human Life

Part II: Your Spirituality in Your Workplace

Part II personalizes the topic through a deeper discussion of spirituality in the workplace in contrast with "faith at work," the risks of "junk-food spirituality," the essential traits of a spiritual person and the specific on-the-job behaviors that result from each trait:

4. The Role of Spirituality at Work

5. Seven Essential Traits of a Spiritual Person

6. Spiritual Behaviors on the Job

Part III: The Ethics of Working It All Out

Part III discusses the indispensable elements of an ethical business; presents the current understandings of corporate social responsibility (CSR) and the debates about its importance; describes the changing concepts of business in the 21st century, including the debates about stockholders vs. stakeholders and ownership vs. stewardship; and includes leadership examples of companies that have won awards for their ethics and their social responsibility. The chapters are:

7. Ethical Elements in Business

8. The Changing Role of Business

9. Corporate Social Responsibility

10. The Global Perspective: Issues in CSR

Part IV: Living Into Your Spiritual Future at Work

Part IV includes the principles for a spiritual workplace, examples of companies that have won awards in this area, and some personal tasks involved in incorporating spirituality into your management practice:

11. The Spiritual Workplace

12. Integrating Spirituality into Leadership and Management

Part V: Additional Resources

The book concludes with four appendixes and an index:

- **Appendix A, Business Awards,** provides information about criteria that various organizations use to select award-winning business in the areas of ethics, CSR, and spirituality.

- **Appendix B, Ethical Elements in Today's Business,** presents information and opinion from the media and the web about real companies facing ethical dilemmas and invites you to consider what ethical decisions you would advise the corporations to make.

- **Appendix C, Troublesome Traits in Human Leaders,** describes some problematic behaviors that are common to leaders and managers in the workplace and that represent their "shadow side" as explained in Chapter 11.

- **Appendix D, Ethics Pledge,** presents an ethical pledge that you are invited to sign.

Personal Applications

Each chapter begins with a story or quotation and ends with questions for reflection or a meditation.

Why I Wrote This Book

With 15 years' experience in Christian education and nearly 20 years working as a technical writer, supervisor, and manager for high tech software companies, I understand the huge gap between spirituality and business. Now I am eager to promote the acceptance and expression of all spiritualities in the workplace, and to encourage discussion and dialogue about work issues in faith communities.

I wrote this book for three reasons. First, I received a personal challenge to address some of the issues in this book. Second, I was driven by my ongoing belief in preserving, respecting, and valuing diversity and pluralism in the workplace. Finally, the available books I surveyed that dealt with Workplace Spirituality were narrowly focused.

My Personal Challenge

The personal challenge came from Peter Morris, host of *The Business Shrink* radio show, who advised me that my website www.WorkplaceSpirituality.info should include what he called "rules of the road," that is, the behavioral specifics of workplace spirituality. I thought about it and decided, "I can do that—I'll write a book!"

A Concern for Pluralism

The second impetus for this *Workplace Spirituality* book was the growth of the "faith at work," movement. This movement is focused on the Christian faith, usually evangelical. *It is very appropriate for Christians to take their faith to work,* but I am concerned that the very fact that Christian evangelicals are taking the initiative may make those of different faiths timid or reluctant to express their own spirituality.

So this book is a simple "course correction" aimed at placing an emphasis on the necessity of religious and spiritual pluralism in the workplace. After all, spirituality in the workplace is another form of diversity for all of us to value in the workplace.

A "Complete" Guide?

The third reason I wrote this book is that other books I have seen on Workplace Spirituality are usually limited to only one aspect of the topic. I do not know of another book that includes the topics of personal spiritual expression and behavior *with* business ethics *and* globally-aware corporate social responsibility, *plus* a picture of a spiritually-friendly workplace *along with* some specific suggestions for making it a reality.

Complete in the title doesn't mean that *Workplace Spirituality: A Complete Guide for Business Leaders* includes every aspect or detail of workplace spirituality you need to learn. But here you will discover all the *essential elements* of workplace spirituality, from personal traits and behaviors to business ethics, from a philosophy of business to corporate social responsibility in a global economy, and from characteristics and principles of a spiritually-friendly workplace to steps you can take to invite spirituality into your workplace.

Think of *complete* as a list of all the broad topics that must be considered for a workplace to be spiritually-friendly.

- Providing a meditation room and opportunities for employees to express their spirituality is not enough. Focusing only on encouraging workers' personal spiritual needs does not relieve a company of its responsibility to conduct its business in a way that protects the environment.

- Being strictly ethical in accounting practices is not enough. Ethical accounting does not free a company from the responsibility of paying a living wage, nor excuse it for discrimination in hiring and promoting.

- Providing access to corporate chaplains is not enough. Making chaplains available to employees in the U.S. does not make up for violating the human rights of immigrants or of overseas workers in the supply chain.

What Can This Book Do For You?

Here you will learn some of the essential traits of spiritual individuals and the job-related behaviors that should result from those traits.

Here you will read about some of the companies that have been recognized for excellence in one or more areas of Workplace Spirituality. Some of the same companies may be failing miserably in another area. Businesses are like human beings in that respect – it is very difficult for any one company to "get it all right."

Here you will learn the underlying business theories and ethical issues that decision-makers face every day. These new understandings will enable you to take new, informed approaches to your work.

Here you will also learn the difference between management and leadership and you will be given some tools to become a spiritual leader in your own workplace.

You have the power to help make your workplace one that is fulfilling and productive, that reduces turnover, and that encourages new ideas and insights from inspired employees.

Endnotes

1 News Release - 8/3/2004.
http://pr.monsterworldwide.com/ireye/ir_site.zhtml?ticker=PR_131001&script=410&layout=-6&item_id=599760

Part I Why Workplace Spirituality and Why Now?

In Chapters 1-3, you will discover:

   4 important definitions and distinctions

   6 factors leading to the movement

   5 factors in the movement's silence

   5 understandings of the significance of work

1   What *IS* Workplace Spirituality?

DAVID AND THE MUSLIM WOMAN

David went home from work one day shortly after 9/11, and told his wife about the Muslim woman who works with him.

She was holding her prayer rug, looking for a safe, quiet, obscure place to pray. No such place was designated in the workplace, so he helped her to find an appropriate place.[1]

᪥᪥᪥᪥᪥᪥᪥᪥᪥᪥᪥᪥᪥᪥᪥᪥᪥᪥᪥᪥᪥᪥᪥᪥᪥᪥᪥᪥᪥᪥᪥᪥

What does spirituality have to do with work and the workplace? More and more, workers are insisting that their spirituality be welcomed in the workplace just as their intelligence is. Like intelligence, our spirituality is part of what we bring with us to work.

Workplace Spirituality refers to the ways we express our spirituality at work. It also encompasses the support we receive in the workplace for our experience of awe, for our personal spirituality, and for making ethical, just decisions.

An increasing number of people who shun the adjective *religious*, are willing to describe themselves as *spiritual*. A report on "Religious Identification in the U.S.,"[2] based on polling data from 2001 and 2002, states:

> Large numbers of American adults are disaffiliating themselves from Christianity and from other organized religions. Since World War II, this process had been observed in other countries, like the U.K., other European countries, Australia, Canada, and New Zealand. But, until recently, affiliation with Christianity had been at a high level—about 87%—and stable in the U.S. . . .[3]

If current trends continue, most adults will not call themselves religious within a few years. Results include:

- About 50% consider themselves religious (down from 54% in 1999)

- About 33% consider themselves "spiritual but not religious" (up from 30%)

- About 10% regard themselves as neither spiritual or religious[4]

We cannot discuss Workplace Spirituality until we agree on our terms, so this chapter begins with four definitions and distinctions on which this book is based.

Then we will discuss six factors that led to the current Workplace Spirituality movement. Next we will present the vision that is the motivation for writing this book.

The chapter concludes with some questions for your reflection and a peek at what's ahead.

Four Definitions and Distinctions

If we use *spirituality* as a metaphor for the life journey we are on, then *religion* is the way or set of directions for many people, but it is only the way, not the destination. Laws, doctrines, dogmas, and rituals are our human attempts to give directions to the journey.

Faith is the map, pointing the way, looking beyond religion, seeing beyond where we are at present.

God, Spirit, Mystery, the source of transcendence—is our destination.

But we must go beyond this somewhat poetic representation and consider some of these terms in more depth.

Spirituality

Spirituality is the inborn desire and ability of every person to seek, know, and respond to the Mystery that I call God but which others may call something else: Spirit, Universe, Energy, Life, etc.

In Christian teaching, every person is created in God's image—*imago Deo*—the image of this ultimate reality. Thus every person is a spiritual being, regardless of his or her religion or lack of religion.

1. **Spirituality at Work** is "an organization of business professionals committed to the awakening of soul at work [and] the transformation of work and the workplace into arenas where life is nourished."[5] Its first assumption is:

   > Divine Mystery or the Holy is real and supports life and wholeness. We want to affirm our experience of the reality of the Divine without narrower definition. Most spiritual traditions agree that the Divine is simply too big for our language; "Divine Mystery" is an expression that acknowledges this while still affirming a greater and deeper Reality.[6]

2. The **International Spirit at Work Award** is given jointly by Spirit at Work: The Professional Association for People Involved with Spirituality in the Workplace,[7] the Spirit in Business Institute;[8] The World Business Academy[9] and the European Baha'i Business Forum.[10] The application for this award defines spirituality as having two dimensions: vertical and horizontal. It describes the vertical dimension as:

   > A desire to transcend the individual ego or personality self. This dimension is experienced as a conscious sense of profound connection to the Universe/God/ Spirit.[11]

3. The **Institute for Management Excellence** lists Seven Principles of Spirituality in the Workplace. The seventh principle states:

   > Your self (small *s*) is the person you are here on this planet. Your Self (capital *S*) is the greater energy of the Universe that connects all of us. Learning about who you are, how you can control your world by changing your attitude, and learning to respect and accept others helps unite us together, strengthening that universal energy that keeps us alive. . . . We recognize that each person has their own beliefs. We respect each individual's belief and their right to hold their beliefs sacred and private.

> Spirituality—as we define it—has no religious component
> or preference; it is a way of expressing more humanity.[12]

4. **Richard Eckersley's work** covers many aspects of whether
life is getting better or worse, including: measures of progress;
the relationships between economic growth, quality of life,
and ecological sustainability; the social determinants of
health and well-being; happiness and life satisfaction; visions
of the future; and youth suicide and other problems.[13]
Eckersley writes:

> Spirituality is a deeply intuitive sense of relatedness or
> connectedness to the world and the universe in which we
> live . . . . [an] understanding of our relationship with the
> Cosmos fosters a sense of deeper purpose, or meaning,
> within ourselves. Spirituality is the intuitive sense of what
> science seeks to explain rationally. . . . Meaning in life
> need not be religious. Many people today find it in the
> pursuit of personal goals—in careers, sport or family, for
> example. But spirituality offers something deeper. It is
> central to the age-old questions about the meaning of life:
> Who am I? Where have I come from? Why am I here? It
> represents the broadest and deepest form of connected-
> ness. It is the most subtle, and so easily corrupted by
> societies, yet perhaps the most powerful. It is the only
> form that transcends our personal circumstances, social
> situation and the material world, and so can sustain us
> through the trouble and strife of mortal existence.[14]

Religion

Religion involves the system of thought and the practice through
which many people express their spirituality. Religion usually includes specific beliefs and worship practices related to a specific understanding or definition of God. Religion is often institutionalized
in an organization, such as a temple or church or mosque or other
institution.

Eckersley contrasts spirituality with religion:

> My definition of that truth, of spirituality, is a deeply intuitive
> sense of relatedness or connectedness to the world and the

universe in which we live. I see religions as social institutions built up around a particular spiritual metaphor, or set of metaphors.

Religions may be socially necessary and desirable to obtain the greatest social and personal benefits from a sense of the spiritual—meaning, fulfilment, virtue. I don't feel my own spirituality is particularly adequate or developed.

On the other hand, religions can be made so rigid and sclerotic by institutional inertia, and by layers of bureaucracy, politics and corruption, that their spiritual core withers. When this happens, they become self-serving institutions lacking any higher purpose; worse, they can become potent ideologies of oppression and abuse.[15]

Deepak Chopra's description of religion is even more critical:

Religion is confining and imprisoning and toxic because it is based on ideology and dogma. But spirituality is redeeming and universal.

– Deepak K. Chopra

Paul T. P. Wong,[16] puts it this way:

Spirituality overlaps with religion with respect to belief in the mystical, transcendental reality, and affirmation of meaning and purpose in the midst of suffering and death. But spirituality does not need to be confined within the structure of any organized religion or a particular set of religious beliefs. In short, spirituality is more inclusive than any faith traditions.[17]

The Religious Tolerance website[18] explains that the root word for *religion* may have been the Latin *religo*, meaning *good faith*, or *ritual*. Or the root word may have been the Latin *"religare"* which means *"to tie fast."* Because of the difficulties in defining religion to satisfy everyone, the website itself settled on the following definition:

Religion is any specific system of belief about deity, often involving rituals, a code of ethics, a philosophy of life, and a worldview.[19]

Spiritual Disciplines or Practices

Spiritual disciplines are those practices that we intentionally take on in order to form our spirituality in a specific direction. For example, in Christian teaching, spiritual disciplines are designed to open us to God's presence, to make us available for closer intimacy with God, to help us discern God's will for our lives, and to cooperate with God's ongoing activity in creating us in the likeness of Christ. Other spiritualities have similar disciplines and practices. Their own interpretation of the purpose and result of those practices may be similar, or it may be quite different.

Spiritual Formation

Spiritual formation consists of all of the experiences—both planned and unplanned—that direct and shape (or form) our spirituality. Spiritual formation includes our childhood experiences and our concepts of God (or Mystery) that result from those experiences. It includes religious instruction—or the lack of religious instruction.

As human beings, we seem to be driven to find language to describe our experience of Mystery. We marvel at spiritual experiences and want to express them to further our own understanding as well as to share them with others. And so we study sacred texts, participate in other classes, and spend time in reflection to help us understand who God is and to help us express our experience of God.

As adults, we can select many of the influences that will form the way in which our spirituality continues to unfold and grow. And we can work and pray to *re*-form spirituality that has been *de*-formed by such influences as abuse or harsh teachings.

Six Factors Leading to the Workplace Spirituality Movement

Spirituality in the workplace is not a single, organized movement but a grassroots movement. More and more, workers are insisting that their spirituality be welcomed in the workplace just as their intelligence is. Like intelligence, our spirituality is part of what we bring with us to work. Several factors triggered the movement:

1. First, the stability of the worker/company relationship broke down as employees were laid off more or less according to economic cycles. At the same time, downsizing left the remaining employees grossly overworked. The mutual trust and loyalty between employee and company were eroded, along with the expectation that the company would take care of its employees. Workers learned they had to be on top of their skills and marketability so that they could find new jobs when they needed to. The nature of work and the implied contract between workers and employers changed significantly, forcing workers to take more control of their own careers.

2. The second factor is the ethical breakdown in corporations and the resulting scandals in Enron and other companies. Workers no longer automatically take pride in being associated with a specific company.

3. A third factor is the increasing demand on workers to put in more and more hours—even to 24/7—at the same salary. This demand has not yet been successfully resisted and changed. According to a 1999 *Business Week* article, professionals at that time were spending an average of 40 hours more per month on the job than previously.[20]

4. The fourth factor is the move from a modern to a post-modern culture. This means we no longer expect all of our answers to come from empirical science. There is a re-spiritualization of culture underway that goes deeper than an attempt to balance the sacred and the secular. Today's spirituality is not a return to pre-Enlightenment spirituality but an integration of the secular and the spiritual into a new world view that is still evolving.

5. A fifth factor is the mid-life introspection of the baby boomers.

6. Finally, the sixth factor is the emerging post-modern world view that is not so quick to compartmentalize the secular and spiritual.

All of these factors have led workers to make some demands of their own. They want to bring their spirituality to work, just as they bring their physical bodies and their minds. They want to trust the ethical standards of their employers, not only in the way they conduct business but also in the way they treat both the physical and social environments. They want to find meaning and purpose in their work.

Valuing Spiritual Diversity at Work

Workplace spirituality is about meaning and fulfillment and also about ethics and values, but it is more than meaningful work or ethical business practices. Most contemporary discussions of Workplace Spirituality include a recognition of *transcendence* as a characteristic of spirituality—a recognition that there is a Mystery that is beyond human intelligence and ordinary experience. Dr. Stephen Sundborg, SJ, President of Seattle University, defines spirituality as "one's lived relationship with mystery."

As human beings, we seek to find language to describe our numinous, non-rational experience of Mystery. When the language we find becomes dogma to be defended, our experience and understanding of God becomes a dangerous topic to bring to the workplace. When our effort to proselytize or evangelize others offends them or makes them uncomfortable, then we have overstepped our rights in the workplace and risked violating their rights.

However, many faiths and spiritualities have similar spiritual disciplines and practices, which they describe in different language and which they interpret differently. Spiritual practices, and the numinous experiences that we seek to preserve through those practices, share a great deal in common across all faiths and spiritualities. The respectful sharing of our different symbols and the expressions used to describe our experiences and practices—in other words sharing our faith, beliefs, and religion—can be enriching to all concerned.

The Vision

For the individual worker, a vision of Workplace Spirituality is a workplace where everyone feels safe and free to practice their own faith, whether through prayer, meditation, dietary rules or clothing, and where each person's unique spirituality is honored as an asset to the workplace. It further involves the transformation of society so that the positive values of spirituality are welcomed as human assets in every workplace, whether the workplace is for-profit, not-for-profit, religious, educational, or service-oriented. These values are common to many ancient and new spiritualities, to the "Religions of the Book," and to other faith expressions originating in the East, the West, and with original peoples.

Additional characteristics of a spiritual workplace are discussed in Chapter 11.

Questions for Reflection

As a movement, spirituality in the workplace does not focus directly on God or theology. Instead, it looks to the morality and ethics that are common to most of the world's religions. It endorses creating sacred space in your cubicle or office. It insists on social responsibility and environmental awareness. It encourages tutoring students, offering yoga in addition to aerobics, and meditating at work (along with an even more recent acceptance of napping at work).

One Dallas-based store tells its workers that they have a moral obligation to provide help to their customers, not just to sell to them. A large business in Atlanta now uses only recycled materials in its work and draws its energy only from renewable sources.

A symposium on business and spirituality is held each spring at Babson College in Boston. Specialized websites are new examples and results of this movement.

1. If workers are spiritually nourished in the workplace, will work become a substitute for faith communities as experienced in churches, synagogues, etc.? How will this affect

family life and community involvement? Will it ease or increase individual isolation? As one writer asked, "Who is this 'spirituality' serving—God or the corporation?"[21]

2. Is spirituality being used to give the person more stamina to work longer in the office and therefore spend less time with spouse and children?

3. Is this religion? New age stuff? Quasi-religion? A substitute for faith? An expanded consciousness? Or is it a movement toward accepting a diversity of religious beliefs, faiths, and practices and valuing their contributions in the workplace?

A *Business Week* article summarizes:

The clashes (between the different views) split along the same lines the country does. On one side of the divide are evangelical Christians, some of whom want Workplace Spirituality to focus on a conservative message about Jesus Christ and who think New Age efforts are demonic. On the other are those who fear the movement is a conspiracy to proselytize everyone into thinking alike. Somewhere in between are the skeptics who think it's yet another one of management's fads, exploiting people's faith to make another dollar.[22]

Looking Ahead

To understand today's trends, we must understand how and when those trends arose. Chapter 2, "Highlights of the Movement," presents a high-level overview of the Workplace Spirituality movement over the past 15 years.

Endnotes

1 Personal experience told to the author.
2 "Religious Identification in the U.S.: Christianity Sinking, 'none of the above' rising," Religious Tolerance.org http://www.religioustolerance.org/chr_prac2.htm (Accessed December 14, 2005)
3 Data from The Graduate Center of the City University of New York American Religious Identification Survey (ARIS) conducted in 2001-FEB to APR.
4 Data from USA Today/Gallup Poll in 2002-JAN
5 "Spirituality at Work: Toward a Deeper Wholeness," http://www.spiritualityatwork.com (Accessed November 29, 2004)
6 http://www.spiritualityatwork.com/assumptions.htm (Accessed November 29, 2004)
7 http://www.spiritatwork.org (Accessed November 29, 2004)
8 http://www.spiritinbusiness.org/new/content/home.php
9 http://www.worldbusiness.org
10 http://www.ebbf.org
11 http://www.worldbusiness.org/partners/ISAW-APPLICATION-2004.pdf (Accessed November 29, 2004)
12 The Institute for Management Excellence http://www.itstime.com/rainbow.htm (Accessed November 29, 2004)
13 Eckersley is a fellow at the National Centre for Epidemiology and Population Health at the Australian National University, Canberra, Australia, where he is working on aspects of progress and well-being. He was previously with the Australia's Commonwealth Scientific and Industrial Research Organisation (CSIRO) Resource Futures Program. http://www.metafuture.org/articlesbycolleagues/Eckersley/Richard_Eckersley_bio.htm   (Accessed November 29, 2004)
14 Eckersley, R. "The view from a cave: science, spirituality and meaning," Ockham's Razor, ABC Radio National, 12 December 1999; http://www.abc.net.au/rn/science/ockham/stories/s72221.htm (Accessed November 29, 2004)
15 Ibid.
16 Dr. Paul T. P. Wong, President of International Network on Personal Meaning (INPM), is Research Director and Professor in the Counselling Psychology Department of Trinity Western University, BC, Canada.
17 Dr. Paul T. P. Wong, "Spirituality and Meaning at Work," September, 2003. http://www.meaning.ca/articles/presidents_column/spirituality_work_sept03.htm (Accessed September 1, 2005)
18 http://www.religioustolerance.org/rel_defn.htm#de (Accessed November 30, 2004)
19 Op. cit. The rest of the essay is quite good. For a variety of web definitions see http://www.google.com/search?hl=en&lr=&oi=defmore&q=define:religion

20 November 1, 1999 cover story: "Religion in the Workplace: The growing presence of spirituality in Corporate America" *Business Week Online*, http://www.businessweek.com/1999/99_44/b3653001.htm (Accessed November 30, 2004)

21 "Spirituality in the Workplace" by Fr. Dér Stépanos Dingilian, Ph.D. © 1999, Armenian Apostolic Church http://www.hopeforfamily.org/sprt_wkplc_01.html (Accessed November 30, 2004)

22 November 1, 1999 cover story: "Religion in the Workplace: The growing presence of spirituality in Corporate America" Business Week Online, http://www.businessweek.com/1999/99_44/b3653001.htm (Accessed November 30, 2004)

TOM SAYS GOOD-BYE TO JESUS

*Tom would talk with Jesus as he drove to work every day.
Then, when he parked the car, he would say, "Well, 'bye Jesus;
see you at five o'clock," and leave him in the car during the
work day.*

Expressing his personal faith at work would be unthinkable.[1]

❦❦

In "Spirituality and Meaning at Work" Paul T. P. Wong writes:

> The movement to bring spirit and soul to business is no passing
> fad; it continues to grow and with no signs of abating. Clearly,
> something significant and enduring is stirring the corporate
> world . . . .[2]

The present spiritual movement is probably the most significant
trend in management since the human-potential movement in the
50s. It appears to be a grassroots movement, as more and more people entertain the notion that work can be meaningful and fulfilling.
In the wake of the Enron debacle, management is also more willing
to take spiritual and moral values seriously.[3]

It is difficult to pin down the beginning of the Workplace Spirituality movement. But the movement was not something that began as
a result of the September 11, 2001 terrorist attacks on the World
Trade Center in New York City. Furthermore, the movement is
world-wide, not limited to the United States.

The proliferation of websites and books devoted to the subject began in the 1990s. This chapter briefly describes the most noticeable
organizations and websites on the subject. It then looks at what has
happened to the initial momentum of the movement since 2001,
and concludes with some questions for your consideration.

Organizations and Websites from 1990 to the Present

The movement has roots and influences from the past, especially
in management theory. It is beyond our scope to investigate those in
detail in this book. However, in October 1999, Marguerite Rigoglioso
quoted Michael Beer, Harvard Business School's Cahners-Rabb Professor of Business Administration, who noted that the movement
was not really new:

> It's really no different from efforts that have been going on for
> decades to create organizations that are more than money-
> making instruments," contends Michael Beer. "We had
> corporate sensitivity training in the 1950s, for example, which
> was all about getting people to communicate better and
> express their feelings. We've had the total quality movement
> and the move toward creating teams and the high-commitment
> workplace. I see what's going on today as simply a reiteration
> of these previous trends. [4]

The following list includes the older organizations but is by no
means exhaustive in listing newer ones.

1. The **Association for Spirit at Work (ASAW)** was
   founded in July 1993 by Judi Neal as a non-profit association
   of people and organizations interested in the study and/or
   practice of spirituality in the workplace. The new vision
   statement of ASAW is:

   > To make a difference in the world by expanding the role
   > of business in transforming society. . . . We will be
   > successful when a critical mass of organizations are
   > committed to caring for the environment, are deeply
   > respectful of local cultures, and are committed to the full

development of all human beings who are connected to or impacted by the organization. We are committed to being an inclusive organization, embracing people from all faith traditions, as well as those who do not practice or adhere to any particular faith or religion.[5]

2. **Seven Principles of Spirituality in the Workplace** [6] was first published in November 1995. At that time, when the founders searched for "Spirituality in the Workplace" on the Internet, no other sites on the topic were listed.

3. The mission of the International Symposium on Spirituality and Business is

To transform commerce and uplift the human spirit in the workplace by fostering principles that successfully integrate ethical practice, environmental responsibility, and social justice in a global economy.[7]

The idea, born in 1996, resulted in the First International Symposium on Spirituality and Business: "Authentic Dialogue and Interfaith Collaboration" held in March 1998 at Andover-Newton Theological School in Newton, Massachusetts. The symposium later moved to Babson College in Wellesley, Massachusetts, where it has continued to be an annual event. The theme of the 7th annual symposium, held in 2004, was "Uplifting the Human Spirit: Tools for Integrating Spirituality into Business."

4. The **Avodah Institute** originated as an educational organization to help leaders integrate the claims of their faith with the demands of their work.

Avodah (Ah´-voe-dah) is a Hebrew word used in the Bible that has two distinct yet intertwined meanings: worship and work. The dual meaning of this ancient word offers powerful wisdom for modern times.[8]

The Institute was co-founded by David Miller, an ordained Presbyterian minister with a PhD in Ethics (and former senior executive in international finance) and C. William Pollard, then chairman and CEO of the ServiceMaster Company.

5. Yale Divinity School's **Center for Faith and Culture** was founded in 2003, with David Miller as executive director. Miller is also Director of the **Ethics and Spirituality in the Workplace** program. He teaches business ethics at Yale Divinity School and the Yale School of Management. The mission of the Yale Center for Faith and Culture is

> To promote the practice of faith in all spheres of life through theological research and leadership develop-ment.[9]

One of the Center's three programs is the Ethics and Spirituality in the Workplace program, which seeks

> To help people integrate the claims of their faith with the demands of their work.

6. In December 1999, a new special interest group on **Management, Spirituality & Religion** was formed by the Academy of Management (AOM), a leading professional association for scholars dedicated to creating and disseminating knowledge about management and organizations.[10]

7. The **Workplace Spirituality** website[11] was established by Nancy Smith in the fall of 2001. Its positioning statement is:

> Expressing spirituality in the workplace through your career calling, ethics, economic justice, spiritual prac-tices, and spiritual values.

Information is divided into six areas: Spirituality in the Workplace as a Movement, Business Ethics and Integrity, Economic and Social Justice, From Career to Calling, Personal Spiritual Practices, and Applying Spiritual Values on the Job.

8. The **Institute for Spirituality and Organizational Leadership** of Santa Clara University's Leavey School of Business, presented "Bridging the Gap between Spirituality and Business," in March 2001."[12] Its purpose is

> To explore issues of spirituality within the context of organizations . . .

The Movement Since 2001

For a while the terms *spirituality* and *spirituality in the workplace* were popular buzzwords. Workplace Spirituality made a big splash in the late 90s and through 2001. There were lots of media articles and lots of excitement. Many new websites were created—some of them excellent but no longer functioning today. An exciting beginning ran into some obstacles:

In the Introduction to *Ethics and Spirituality at Work:Hopes and Pitfalls of the Search for Meaning in Organizations,* Thierry C. Pauchant PhD, Professor in management at HEC Montreal and consulting faculty at the Fielding Graduate Institute, Santa Barbara, points out the pitfalls wrote:

> Integrating ethics and spirituality into all facets of management and leadership of organizations has become an urgent need expressed by managers themselves. How to reconcile economic value and ethical or spiritual value becomes the fundamental question. This is a fascinating, serious and slippery subject. The potential pitfalls are numerous: ethics can devolve into legalism, dogmatism or abusive moralisation; spirituality can lead to fundamentalism, archaic superstitions or the growth of abusive sects; and both ethics and spirituality can be co-opted to manipulate people, employees and managers as a way to maximize profits.[13]

Five Factors in the Movement's Silence

There are five important reasons why we haven't heard much about Workplace Spirituality in the media in the early years of the twenty-first century.

1. First, the severe unemployment since 2001 has made job-seekers less assertive. They have often been thankful for any job and spiritual fulfillment has taken a back seat to financial survival. A recovery here will bring a resurgence in worker demands for spirituality in the workplace.

2. Second, many companies have incorporated some features of the spirituality in the workplace movement—such as ethical

codes and value statements—without using the term spiritual or spirituality. They also continue to give lip service to cooperation and team building—terms that have been part of corporate vocabulary for decades but not always put into practice. And they may even have brought in a yoga instructor as well as some health programs in relaxation and other mind-body practices. This doesn't meet the need or the description of spirituality in the workplace, however.

3. A third, related reason is that some companies have associated spirituality with the New Age Movement and have either embraced that movement as spirituality or have intentionally avoided any connection with it.

4. Fourth, "Spiritual Management Development (SMD)" sees religion as:

    > a dimension of social experience, rather than as an isolated institution. This enables us to understand all work organizations, which use symbolic action to build feelings about meaning, purpose and existence, as potential sites of implicit religion.[14]

    Some SMD training that is offered distorts the meaning of Workplace Spirituality into a mere tool for managers to use to motivate and possibly even manipulate their employees. This kind of training co-opts the term "spiritual" without addressing many of the essential features of what spirituality includes, such as respect for the contribution of each employee's individual spiritual perspective or the ethical responsibilities of corporations.

5. Finally, Faith in the workplace," sometimes called the Faith at Work movement, has taken the spotlight away from spirituality in the workplace. Faith in the workplace does not usually mean the same thing. Some Christians have used the spirituality in the workplace theme to bring an evangelical focus into many workplaces, seeking to win people to Christ. While this is understandable from their perspective, it is not the same thing as respecting and encouraging all forms of spirituality. *Certainly we who are Christians have our place at the table*

and our spiritual contribution to make. The risk lies in violating what spirituality in the workplace is all about.

Questions for Reflection

1. Is the movement just a maneuver on the part of businesses to get their workers even more dedicated to the workplace, more willing to work even longer hours, and more willing to give up time that might otherwise be spent in recreation, with family, in community or charitable work, or in religious practice?

2. If a company is based on noble principles, will it feel more self-righteous when layoffs come?

3. Is the workplace where people should be looking for spiritual fulfillment? Can business deliver? Or should it avoid trying to meet spiritual needs and simply allow individual spiritual expression while protecting the rights and needs of all in the workplace?

Looking Ahead

Chapter 3, "The Purpose of Work in Human Life," discusses five different spiritual perspectives on work.

Endnotes

1   Personal experience told to the author.
2   Dr. Paul T. P. Wong, "Spirituality and Meaning at Work," September, 2003. http://www.meaning.ca/articles/presidents_column/spirituality_work_sept03.htm (Accessed September 1, 2005)
3   *Ibid.*
4   Marguerite Rigoglioso, "Spirit at Work: The Search for Deeper Meaning in the Workplace," Harvard Business School *Working Knowledge,* October 12, 1999, http://hbswk.hbs.edu/item.jhtml?id=644&t=organizations&noseek=one (Accessed December 2, 2004)

5   http://www.spiritatwork.org/aboutSAW/aboutus.htm   (Accessed December 3, 2004)

6   http://www.itstime.com/rainbow.htm (Accessed December 3, 2004)

7   http://www3.babson.edu/Events/spiritualityandbusiness/About-Us.cfm (Accessed December 3, 2004)

8   http://www.avodahinstitute.com/ (Accessed December 3, 2004)

9   http://www.yale.edu/faith/about/mission.html   (Accessed December 3, 2004)

10 http://aom.pace.edu/msr/

11 http://www.WorkplaceSpirituality.info

12 http://business.scu.edu/spirituality_leadership/default.htm   (Accessed February 28, 2006)

13 Thierry C. Pauchant., "Introduction," *Ethics and Spirituality at Work:Hopes and Pitfalls of the Search for Meaning in Organizations* (Quorum Books, 2002)

14 Emma Bell and Scott Taylor, "From Outward Bound to Inward Bound: Affective Management," paper presented to the Emotion and Spirituality in Organizations Track, Second European Academy of Management Conference, Stockholm School of Entrepreneurship, University of Stockholm, Sweden, May 9-11, 2002, p. 2

3   The Purpose of Work in Human Life

TIME TO LEARN

A young but earnest Zen student approached his teacher, and asked the Zen Master:

"If I work very hard and diligent how long will it take for me to find Zen?"

The Master thought about this, then replied, "Ten years."

The student then said, "But what if I work very, very hard and really apply myself to learn fast—How long then?"

Replied the Master, "Well, twenty years."

"But, if I really, really work at it. How long then?" asked the student.

"Thirty years," replied the Master.

"But, I do not understand," said the disappointed student. "At each time that I say I will work harder, you say it will take me longer. Why do you say that?"

Replied the Master, "When you have one eye on the goal, you only have one eye on the path." [1]

  To find joy in your work is the greatest thing for a human being.

Harry Roberts [2]

It seems that we humans, at least in the United States, have very ambivalent feelings about work. Some of our views of work originate with the Jewish and Christian scriptures, which present work as both blessing and curse.

Buddhism gives us the concept of Right Livelihood, the traditional term for "work that is ethical and helpful to one's spiritual development."[3]

In this chapter we will examine an overview of five concepts of work. The chapter concludes with some questions for your reflection and a peek at what's ahead.

Work as Good and Natural Activity

> Let us realize that the privilege to work is a gift, that power to work is a blessing, that love of work is success.
> – David O. McKay[4]

In the first chapter of Genesis, God is at work creating the universe and everything in it. God calls it all good and takes satisfaction in the results. In fact, Sabbath is a time for God to enjoy what God has created.

God creates human beings and invites them to participate by caring for creation. Work is a natural activity:

> And the Lord God planted a garden in Eden, in the east; and there he put the man whom he had formed . . . . The Lord God took the man and put him in the garden of Eden to till it and keep it.
> – Genesis 2:8, 15

Work is one place we look for meaning. Not all work is meaningful, and work should not be our only source of meaning. But performing meaningful work, whether for pay or not, contributes significantly to how we feel about ourselves as well as to our overall sense of well-being. St. Benedict of Nursia (480-543), the founder of western monasticism, recognized that fact in saying, "Idleness is the enemy of the soul."[5]

Norvene Vest paraphrases St. Benedict's statement to read, "Work is the friend of the soul."[6]

Work grounds us in reality. Sigmund Freud said that work "attaches the individual ... firmly to reality" because it "gives him a secure place in a portion of reality, in the human community."[7]

This anchoring characteristic of work is important in the *Rule* of St. Benedict. In the *Rule*, work is conducive to holiness and so is seen as a holy endeavor, with prayer it is the chief characteristic:

> Human work is meant to be a holy endeavor. . . . one of the means by which we love and serve God instead of something separate and accidental to our faith.[8]

Work as Curse or Punishment

> Work is a necessary evil to be avoided.
> — Mark Twain

> With labour you shall win your food . . . You shall gain your bread by the sweat of your brow.
> — Genesis 3:19[9]

From Genesis 3:17-19 some people get the idea that work itself is punishment. A careful study of the text shows that because of their disobedience to God, Adam and Eve are told that the *process* of performing work will become difficult and painful. The reality of work has already been blessed by God.

Still, much of work as we experience it is frustrating, unfulfilling, and dehumanizing:

> Work is, by its very nature, about violence—to the spirit as well as to the body. It is about ulcers as well as accidents, about shouting matches as well as fistfights, about nervous breakdowns as well as kicking the dog around. It is, above all (or beneath all), about daily humiliations. To survive the day is triumph enough for the walking wounded among the great many of us.[10]

Work as Calling

> To fulfill a dream, to be allowed to sweat over lonely labor, to be given a chance to create, is the meat and potatoes of life. The money is the gravy.
>
> – Bette Davis

Other texts indicate that work is a creative activity, a partnership of co-creating with God, and a calling or vocation.

> Why do you spend . . . your labor for that which does not satisfy?
>
> –Isaiah 55:1-2

Writing on Benedictine spirituality, Norvene Vest says:

> Many of us harbor some form of this vision: a deep, often unspoken sense that we have been created for a special purpose, that we have a serious and holy calling to be expressed through active engagement with the world around us—that is, through our work.[11]

The word *vocation* comes from a Latin term meaning invitation, or calling. The word *voice* comes from the same root. Originally it meant that God calls you specifically to the work that you should be doing.

> It is well for a man to respect his vocation whatever it is, and to think himself bound to uphold it, and claim for it the respect it deserves.
>
> – Charles Dickens

Common usage today has reduced the meaning of *vocation* to "the particular occupation for which you are trained" or "a body of people doing the same kind of work" or a trade learned in a vocational school. Too often the sense of *calling* is missing.

Many contemporary books and articles, both spiritual and secular, are written to help us discover our vocation—that inner calling that is most satisfying to us. One of the most beautiful definitions of vocation is by Frederick Buechner:

The place God calls you is the place where your deep gladness and the world's deep hunger meet.[12]

Work as Right Livelihood

Right Livelihood *(ajiva)* means to earn one's living in a simple, unpretentious, morally correct way. And it means that any wealth should be gained legally, as well as peacefully . . . . earning a living in a way that is not harmful to other sentient beings.[13]

– The Noble Eightfold Path of Chan Buddhism

Among the characteristics of Right Livelihood are the following:

• Right Livelihood does no harm.

To be *Right Livelihood* according to Buddhist teaching, your work should not harm or exploit other people or the environment.

A job selling lottery tickets, liquor and cigarettes in a liquor store probably would not meet this standard because the products being sold are likely to harm or exploit other people. If this is the best you can do to meet short-term needs, is it ethical to perform this job or should you refuse to work?

On the other hand, virtually every job in our society has ethical implications. In our complex society, we seldom know if the food products we sell in the supermarket—or buy for our own consumption—are owned by conglomerates that also produce cigarettes. We don't know if the materials we help manufacture are sold to companies that make military weapons. We don't know if the CEOs of the corporations we work for are involved in bribes to politicians or drug dealers or giving or receiving political favors. We often don't know if our favorite discount store has unfair labor policies or imports products made with the labor of exploited people in developing nations. It's impossible to be totally pure in all our ethical choices and decisions.

What dilemmas would each of us face if we gathered all the facts about our potential or current employers?

- Right Livelihood expresses your identity and calling.

  To be Right Livelihood, your work should come from within you and give you satisfaction. It does not have to be your "perfect job"—there is no such thing—nor does it have to be your life-long career. The work that you do as Right Livelihood may change throughout your life, just as your calling may change. In fact, both of these probably *will* change. In the Benedictine tradition, our work is one of the principal means for discovering our own gifts and needs. We discover and become who we are through what we do—that is why work is a friend of the soul.[14]

- Right Livelihood contributes to the common good.

  To be Right Livelihood, your work should contribute to society in a positive way and connect you with the rest of life and the world.

  Your work is to discover your work and then with all your heart to give yourself to it.

  – The Buddha [15]

Work as Spiritual Path

If you choose to see it that way, your work can be a spiritual path. . . . The stage of Right Livelihood seems to come as a gift. The individual has a strong sense of what work to do that will nourish her spirit and will allow her to be of service. . . . Right Livelihood is often the driving force behind the urge to be an entrepreneur; the ability to create a workplace that is not in conflict with deeply held values, and that can be nurturing and supportive of spiritual principles such as service, compassion, and empathy.[16]

In the words of Kahlil Gibran, "Work is love made visible."[17]

Mindfulness/Contemplation

Mindfulness is a state of being in which you are focused on the present moment and on the task you are performing in the present. In Buddhist teaching, Right Livelihood is work that you can learn to perform with mindfulness.

> The word "mindfulness" can be explained as a combination of "bare attention" and "clear comprehension". The purpose pf practicing mindfulness is to see things as they really are, unswayed by aversion or attraction.[18]

Mindfulness involves staying aware of your responsibilities and paying close attention to them. It includes awareness, attentiveness, and care. Learning mindfulness, therefore, furthers your personal spiritual growth:

> You don't need to be too identified with what you do. We think what we do is who we are. [But] when you die you aren't going to be who you are, you're going to be something else, or when you get sick, or when things change around, or when the earthquake comes, or whatever, what you do isn't going to matter a lot; it's something that you do. You can do it instead in a spirit of adventure or a dance or an exploration . . . . Growth and awareness means that we can begin to use our work, whatever it is, to wake up, to awaken.[19]

Benedictine spirituality describes this kind of awareness as

> A way of seeing, a contemplative attitude facilitated by a practice of awareness and reflection on God's presence revealed in every encounter . . . . Work punctuated by prayer enables both to become vehicles for the natural emergence of deep insights about God.[20]

Brother David Steindl-Rast prefers the word *wholeheartedness* because it

> expresses better what mindfulness as a technical term means; that you respond to every situation from your center, from your heart—that you listen with your heart to every situation, and your heart elicits the response. [21]

Connection to community

Connection to life and to community is essential to both Right Livelihood and the meaning of spirituality itself. Work that does not support such connection is contradictory to both:

> In a nutshell, [Right Livelihood] is honest work that matches one's personal values, contributes to the good of the community, does not cause a person undue stress, and allows one to live a whole and balanced life. Right livelihood is focused on making a life rather than making a killing.[22]

Search for meaning

> Meaning in life need not be religious. Many people today find it in the pursuit of personal goals—in careers, sport or family, for example. But spirituality offers something deeper. It is central to the age-old questions about the meaning of life: Who am I? Where have I come from? Why am I here? It represents the broadest and deepest form of connectedness.[23]

One of the risks inherent in the Workplace Spirituality movement is the tendency by some to expect work to encompass *all* of the meaning in our lives, including leisure, spiritual formation, and faith expressions. Benjamin Hunnicutt, author and professor at the University of Iowa explained in a lecture:

> I am convinced that our new modern religion is work; our daily sacrifice, our jobs. Work itself, and the things we have made, from buildings to bridges, to academic "bodies of knowledge," are the object of our worship and ultimate loyalties. Work, and the works of our hands are where we live and move and have our being.[24]

This is made clearer when we consider how our concept of leisure has changed, especially in the United States. In his book *Work Without End: Abandoning Shorter Hours for the Right to Work*, Hunnicutt relates the rise of consumerism to our change from using leisure to be more human to using leisure as a time to escape from being human.[25]

Questions for Reflection

1. We have explored the idea of work as a good and natural activity, as a curse or punishment, as calling, as Right Livelihood, and as spiritual path. Which best describes your own beliefs about work?

2. Let's take these ideas a step further. Matthew Fox,[26] founder, president emeritus and teaching professor at the University of Creation Spirituality in Oakland, California, says:

   > A question everybody has to ask at work is what is the bottom line? What am I willing to be fired for? What am I willing to die for? I can speak of that not just from theory. In the midst of writing *The Reinvention of Work*, I received a pink slip from the Vatican. Every one of us has to have a conscience. Because work is so influential in the world and affects morality at so many levels, every one of us has to be willing to lose our job over something we believe in.[27]

Looking Ahead

Chapter 4, "The Role of Spirituality at Work," deals with the risks of religion and the advantages of spirituality at work and warns against "junk food" spirituality.

Endnotes

1   A Classic Zen Story on Learning Enlightenment, The Story Bin, http://www.storybin.com/sponsor/sponsor100.shtml (Accessed January 3, 2006)
2   Agronomist, cowboy, woodworker, welder, boxer, gun-sight maker, spiritual teacher in the Native American tradition, and Ginger Rogers's dance partner. Quoted by Lewis Richmond in *Work as a Spiritual Practice: A Practical Buddhist Approach to Inner Growth and Satisfaction on the Job* (Broadway, 2000)
3   See http://www.fwbo.org/rightlivelihood.html (Accessed October 9, 2004)
4   Ninth President of The Church of Jesus Christ of Latter-day Saints, b. September 8, 1873, d. January 18, 1970

5 *Rule of Benedict*, Chapter 48 "Of the Daily Work"
   http://www.kansasmonks.org/RuleOfStBenedict.html#ch48 (Accessed December 1, 2004)
6 Vest, Norvene, *Friend of the Soul: A Benedictine Spirituality of Work* (Cambridge, MA: Cowley Publications, 1997)
7 Sigmund Freud, *Civilization and its Discontents*, (New York:W.W. Norton & Co., 1962)
8 Vest, *op. cit.*, p. 4
9 Genesis 3:19, *New English Bible,* (Oxford University Press and Cambridge University Press, 1970)
10 Studs Terkel, *Working: People Talk About What They Do All Day and How They Feel About What They Do* (NY:Pantheon Books, 1972), p. xi
11 Vest, *op. cit.*, p. 3
12 Frederick Buechner, *Wishful Thinking: A Theological ABC,* HarperSanFrancisco; Rev/Expand edition (September 24, 1993)
13 http://www.thedailylama.com/Lib/livelihood.html
14 Vest, *op. cit.*, p. 44
15 Hindu Prince Gautama Siddharta, the founder of Buddhism, 563-483 B.C.
16 *The Four Gateways to Spirit at Work,* unpublished writing by Dr. Judith Neal, http://www.fourgateways.com/uversity/chaptertwo.htm (Accessed September 23, 2004)
17 Gibran, Kahlil, *The Prophet* (Knopf, 1923)
18 http://buddhism.about.com/library/weekly/aa082402a.htm (Accessed October 9, 2004)
19 Householder Series by Jack Kornfield: The Eightfold Noble Path—Right Livelihood http://www.mandala.hr/8/hh5.html (Accessed October 9, 2004)
20 Vest, *op. cit.*, p. 4-5
21 Brother David Steindl-Rast, O.S.B., "All in the Same Boat" http://www.gratefulness.org/readings/dsr_SameBoat3.htm (Accessed January 4, 2006)
22 Andersen, John O., "Could Right Livelihood be a Better Choice Than Early Retirement?" http://www.spiritone.com/~andersen/rightliv.html (Accessed October 9, 2004)
23 Eckersley, R. "The view from a cave: science, spirituality and meaning," Ockham's Razor, ABC Radio National, 12 December 1999; http://www.abc.net.au/rn/science/ockham/stories/s72221.htm (Accessed November 29, 2004)
24 Benjamin Hunnicutt, "Finding God at Iowa" Lecture: "Death and Work; Memory and Leisure," September 5, 2003 http://www.uiowa.edu/~lsa/bkh/Geneva.htm (Accessed October 9, 2005)
25 Temple University Press, reprint edition August, 1990. See also Linda Marks in "The Loss of Leisure in a Culture of Overwork" http://www.ofspirit.com/lindamarks12.htm (Accessed October 9, 2005)
26 Lecturer and author of 26 books, a member of the Dominican Order for 34 years, Matthew Fox was expelled from his order in 1991 for his teachings by Cardinal Ratzinger (now Pope Benedict XVI), who was then head of the Congregation of Doctrine and Faith (formerly called the Office of the Holy Inquisition).

27 "Beyond a Job: Doing the Great Work," An Interview with Matthew Fox by
Mary Nurrie Stearns on "Personal Transformation," website,
http://64.233.187.104/search?q=cache:cWtljKs690gJ:www.personal
transformation.com/Fox.html+Matthew+Fox+on+work&hl=en (Accessed
January 3, 2006)

Part II   Your Spirituality in Your Workplace

Chapters 4-6 challenge you to consider the following personally:

> **The risks of religion and the advantages of spirituality**

> **7 essential traits of a spiritual person, including:**

>> **3 traits in the Circle of Being**

> **4 traits in the Circle of Connection**

> **Job behaviors from each of the 7 traits**

4   The Role of Spirituality
at Work

TRANSFORMING WORK

Recalling his early days at the company, Walter told me about being genuinely enthusiastic and trying to exert his creativity. Then the work took on a plodding, mind-numbing cadence, he said. "Do this," "Do that," day after day. He followed his marching orders, and before long, he was beginning each workday by checking his brain at the door.

Then things changed dramatically. Walter got a new supervisor who seemed keenly aware that the employees in production were real human beings. On Walter's 20th anniversary with the company, the supervisor asked him how he wanted to be honored for reaching the milestone. The veteran employee surprised everyone with this response: "Let me visit a customer plant."

For two decades, Walter worked in a foundry, producing castings for power-generating facilities. His work helped create 12-cylinder crankcases, electric motor housings, and 300-pound manifolds. Yet in all that time, he never got to see the finished product doing its thing at a customer site. In 40,000 hours of work, he had never, ever seen the final fruits of his labor.

The supervisor heard the request and understood. And a month later, Walter was flying halfway across the country to visit one of their major customers. He spent a full week there—touring several plants, seeing the castings in action, and getting into conversations about foundry stuff like flaskless molds, drag molding, and integrated cleaning.

When he returned, Walter seemed to have undergone a trans-formation. There was a lift to his comments, a certain spirit of engagement. He told me all about the trip, about the briefing he did for his coworkers soon after his return, and about the company's plans to institute regular customer trips. He went on about all the ideas he had picked up at the customer plant for making good castings even better.

The story has a happy ending for Walter. But cynicism lives on in so many other organizations. Plenty of workplaces have tried to become mission-driven, but nurturing a true mission requires so much more.[1] — From The Blossoming of a Workplace Drone byTom Terez

~~~~~~

Work is brutal. Work is a four-letter word . . . . But if we bring our souls to work, then we can transform our work. That is when our work can begin to transform us. The problem for most people is that their work transforms them into something bad, something bitter and tired and broken.[2]

– Tim McGuire

~~~~~~

Spirituality in the workplace—in contrast to a faith-based work-place where a specific religion is the supposed norm—has a positive effect on workers. Spirituality is not the same thing as religion. Spiri-tuality is a more inclusive term. Like personality and intelligence, spirituality is part of what makes us human. It should be part of what we bring with us to work. The company and our co-workers will benefit from having the whole person at work.

Some people express their spirituality through faith and religion. But others are spiritual without being religious. Both groups of peo-ple should be encouraged to express their spirituality and to use it as the basis of their interpersonal behavior and ethical decisions.

We will begin by exploring the risks of *religion* at work and con-tinue with a discussion of the advantages of *spirituality* at work. Then we will present a detailed discussion on "junk-food" spirituality. The chapter concludes with some questions for your reflection and a peek at what's ahead.

The Risks of Religion at Work

> Religion is about rituals and morals and systems, all of them good but all of them incomplete. Spirituality is about coming to consciousness of the sacred in the secular.[3]

Too often religion is seen as

> A system of rewards, blackmail, calculation, and aggrandizement, in which people come off only best or worst . . . . Perfectionism uncovers those compulsions that drive us to bring into being a tyrannical, idealized self.[4]

Psychoanalyst Karen Horney (1885-1952) identified three common human coping styles. In his book *Soul Making: The Desert Way of Spirituality*, Dr. Alan W. Jones, Dean of Grace Cathedral in San Francisco, CA, explains Horney's coping styles and how religion often takes them to unhealthy extremes:

1. The first coping style is *compliance*, which Horney also referred to as the *moving-toward* strategy or *the self-effacing solution*. Under the guise of an unquestioning understanding of the religious command to "be ye perfect," this coping style can become an attitude and demeanor of saintliness and forbearance that repels others. The extreme is perfectionism.

2. The second coping style is *aggression*, which Horney also referred to as the *moving-against* strategy or *the expansive solution*. An unquestioning belief in religious authority can turn this strategy into a sense of heroism as the believer, like a knight of old, bravely and courageously defends the Truth. The extreme manifests itself in ambition and revenge.

3. The third coping style is *withdrawal*, which Horney also referred to as the *moving-away-from* strategy or *the resigning solution*. Under a religion that is more vengeful than life-enhancing, this

strategy leads to an aloofness that masquerades as wisdom and self-sufficiency

It is a short path from perfectionism to self-righteousness, from a commitment to holiness or righteousness to a cruel vindictiveness in defending the honor of one's God, from an unquestioning acceptance of revealed truth to the manipulation of others for their own good.[5]

Those of us most committed to our religious faith need to be the most diligent in examining our own motives and our own openness to personal and spiritual growth.

The Advantages of Spirituality at Work

I think it's now permissible to say, "This is who I am. This is what I believe." I'm hearing it more in the workplace. I'm hearing more about ethics in the workplace. I think businesses are also very concerned that they don't signal you can use your belief in God instead of rational management procedures. And religion tends to push for never-enough solutions of its own. So what everyone is searching for is a framework for success that goes beyond money and goes to these lasting values. It's not just people with one sectarian belief.[6]

Rabbi Michael Lerner challenges us to "Come out of the closet as a spiritual person. Affirm it publicly."[7]

Unlike many religions, spirituality does not focus on dogma or theology. When the language we use to express our spiritual experience goes beyond sharing who we are and becomes dogma to be defended, or results in aggressive proselytizing, then our spirituality becomes a dangerous topic to bring to the workplace.

At its best, Workplace Spirituality looks to the morality and ethics that are common to most of the world's religions. It accepts and values a diversity of spiritual expressions, religious beliefs, faiths, and practices in the workplace. It allows and encourages such things as: creating sacred space in your cubicle or office, social responsibility, environmental awareness, tutoring students, yoga, and meditating at work.

Dr. Anthony T. Padovano describes Americans as being in "bondage to cultural obsessions, hidden persuaders and frenetic compulsions."[8] What could fit that description better than the "cultural obsessions" we have about work, the "hidden persuaders" in advertising, and our "frenetic compulsions" to do everything possible to win the approval of others, especially at work?

A *fear of imperfection* underlies our attempts to measure up to some ill-defined standard and results in excessive activity on our part. We experience this in our pressured, frantic performance as we "attack" whatever task is before us. This fear is based on the illusion that this time we *can* do it perfectly. But Padovano comments, "There is something belligerent about frenetic action." We seem to be trying to force meaning into our lives.

The *fear of scarcity*, which is based on greed and vanity, manifests itself in excessive consumerism, which feeds the need to earn more and more money. We buy things we don't need or even enjoy. We do this because we seek security and superiority in what we can purchase. Padovano says, "A desperate need to possess is a form of violence. Excessive spending is a sign that one seeks the meaning of life in things."

A study by Ian Mitroff and Elizabeth Denton revealed:

> People are hungry for ways in which to practice spirituality in the workplace without offending their coworkers or causing acrimony. They believe strongly that unless organizations learn how to harness the "whole person" and the immense spiritual energy that is at the core of everyone, they will not be able to produce world-class products and services.[9]

In their research, Mitroff and Denton came to associate spirituality with a desire for meaning. When they asked people where they found the greatest meaning and purpose at work, their top seven responses were:[10]

- The ability to realize my full human potential as a person.
- Being associated with a good or ethical organization.
- Interesting work.
- Making money.

- Having good colleagues; serving humankind.
- Service to future generations.
- Service to my immediate community.

In his column on "Spirituality and Meaning at Work," Wong explains the role of spirituality at work in more detail:

> Spirituality should not be used as a religious garment or a marketing tool. It is concerned with substance rather than image. More specifically, it has to do with how we define ourselves, view the world, relate to others, and make ethical/moral decisions. Here are some of the attributes of spirituality within the context of work:
>
> - Defining ourselves as having inherent values, greater than our roles, titles and possessions
> - Affirming meaning and purpose in spite of absurdity and chaos
> - Emphasizing authenticity, inner wisdom, creativity and transformation
> - Recognizing the immaterial, transcendental, sacred dimensions of reality
> - Having a servant's attitude towards work and leadership
> - Embodying spiritual values of integrity, honesty, love, kindness and respect
> - Emphasizing social responsibility toward the community, society and environment
> - Viewing God and spiritual principles as the grounding for moral decisions[11]

"Junk Food" Spirituality

The other side of the coin of bringing your spirituality into the workplace is bringing your intelligence into your spirituality. We prefer to be immature and have an authority—whether in a person, or book or dogma—tell us what to believe. Naïve and unquestioning acceptance of such an authority leads to a judgmental and vindictive fundamentalism that does violence to others as well as to the believer.

We may resist our desire for the comfort of a soothing authority and, instead, seek some path that will make us feel good. Looking only inside ourselves for answers can degenerate into an unhealthy self-indulgence and self-centered narcissism.

The result is what I call "junk food spirituality."

According to a 1999 USA Today/CNN/Gallup Poll of religious beliefs, "Self-defined spirituality is replacing . . . a church-based faith . . . ." I understand those who reject traditional faiths for all kinds of reasons—their patriarchy, their disregard for the earth, their ignorance of mystery, their claims of inerrancy, etc. Some "New Age" beliefs are attempts to revive lost values in the Old Religions and the beliefs of indigenous peoples.

Today's Workplace Spirituality movement contributes to this phenomenon of eclecticism because it not only emphasizes the common spirituality in all humans (which is good), but often appears to water down all examples of spirituality to the least common denominator (which is not so good).

Faith-free spirituality contains just enough truth to be very tempting. Consider the terms I see in motivational articles from people who want to be published on my website:

- Manifest

- Abundance

- Prosperity thinking

- Create your own destiny

- Believe in yourself

- Self-talk

- Befriend the universe

From the past but still popular is *The Power of Positive Thinking* by Norman Vincent Peale, which teaches:

1. How to eliminate that most devastating handicap—self doubt

2. How to free yourself from worry, stress, and resentment

3. How to climb above problems to visualize solutions and then attain them

4. Simple prayerful exercises that you can do every day, throughout the day, to reinforce your new-found habit of happiness

A more contemporary book is *If It's Going to Be, It's Up to Me* by Robert H. Schuller, which presents his eight principles of "Possibility Thinking," including tapping into "dynamic divine energy."

All of these phrases represent valid concepts, but taken alone, they are not enough. I look to see what the author's *world view* is and, if none is explicit, I become suspicious. Some phrases (such as those made famous by Peale and Schuller) have their solid foundation in Christianity. Some have a foundation in other faiths, in psychology, or in some other world view. I may disagree with some of the world views, but at least there is a foundation beyond the individualistic words used in the expressions.

The 1999 USA Today/CNN/Gallup Poll goes on to say: "Almost one-third regarded themselves as spiritual but not religious, electing to pick and choose belief systems."

That's a nice-sounding cafeteria approach—but without some kind of world view foundation, it may soon lead to the "junk-food" results:

- Without a consistent, coherent foundation, junk-food spirituality consists of empty platitudes that will fall apart as soon as you experience a major catastrophe in health or personal finance. Positive self-talk and belief in yourself lead to blaming yourself when such catastrophes occur.

- Without a consistent, coherent foundation, junk-food spirituality provides a self-absorption that lacks a basis for ethical behavior. By itself, it leads to "looking out for No. 1."

- Without a consistent, coherent foundation, junk-food spirituality lacks a concern for the common good and fails to provide tools for teamwork or community-building.

- Without a consistent, coherent foundation, junk-food spirituality provides no explanation for, or understanding of, suffering. Thus it lacks a motive for compassion, service, sacrifice—or global economic justice.

Beware of the dangers of eclecticism. *Eclecticism* is defined in philosophy as

> The selection of elements from different systems of thought, without regard to possible contradictions between the systems. Eclecticism differs from *syncretism*, which tries to combine various systems while resolving conflicts . . . . Eclectics are frequently charged with being inconsistent, and the term is sometimes used pejoratively.[12]

Reject the mistakes and excesses of traditional religions if you must. Seek what we may have lost in the Old Religions or in native spiritualities if that is your inclination. But be sure that in developing your personal spirituality you look for a total world view. Get the whole meal and don't settle for junk food that tastes good for the moment but has little lasting value.

An Exercise for Your Personal Reflection

Complete the following sentences:

- My life has the most meaning when . . .
- My life has the most energy when . . .
- My life has the most hope when . . .
- When I listen to my own inner being . . .
- I feel most drained of energy when . . .

What do your answers reveal to you about your spirituality?

Looking Ahead

Chapter 5, "Seven Essential Traits of a Spiritual Person," presents three traits that form a *Circle of Being* because they relate to who you are within yourself. The chapter then presents four traits that form a *Circle of Connection* because, taken together, they feed your sense of connectedness to life, the world, other people, and transcendent reality (God/Spirit/Universe).

Endnotes

1   Tom Terez, "The Blossoming of a Workplace Drone," *Workforce Management* (May 2001). Copyright Crain Communications, Inc. Tom Terez is a speaker, workshop leader, and author of the book *22 Keys to Creating a Meaningful Workplace*. See BetterWorkplace Now.com and TomTerez.com.

2   Tim J. McGuire, former editor of the *Minneapolis Star Tribune*, Catholic layman and author of the syndicated column called "More Than Work," dedicated to values and faith in the workplace. Quoted in "The Importance of Spirituality in the Workplace" by Terry Mattingly for Catholic Exchange: http://www.catholicexchange.com/vm/PFarticle.asp?vm_id=2&art_id=16420&sec_id=30503 (Accessed November 5, 2004)

3   "Contemplation in the Midst of Chaos" by Sr. Joan Chittister January 20, 2002 http://www.30goodminutes.org/csec/sermon/Chittister_4513.htm#anchor610088 (Accessed November 5, 2004)

4   Alan Jones, *Soul Making: The Desert Way of Spirituality*, (HarperSanFrancisco, 1985) p. 35

5   *Ibid.*, p. 39-40

6   Laura Nash, an expert in workplace ministry who teaches courses on management and corporate ethics at the Harvard Business School, on NBC-TV's *Today Show*, 19 March 2004 http://www.yale.edu/faith/news/nbc-20040319.html

7   In public speaking, including at the Network of Spiritual Progressives Conference, July 5, 2005, http://www.witherspoonsociety.org/2005/network_of_spiritual_progressives.htm (Accessed March 6, 2006) Lerner is author of *The Left Hand of God: Taking Our Country Back from the Religious Right* (HarperSanFrancisco, 2006) and editor of *Tikkun* Magazine.

8   Anthony T. Padovano, *A Retreat With Thomas Merton: Becoming Who We Are* (Saint Anthony Messenger Press and Franciscan, 1955)

9   "A Study of Spirituality in the Workplace" by Ian Mitroff and Elizabeth Denton, Sloan Management Review, Summer 1999. pp. 83-84, now in book format in *A Spiritual Audit of Corporate America*.

10 *Ibid.*

11 Dr. Paul T. P. Wong, "Spirituality and Meaning at Work," September, 2003. http://www.meaning.ca/articles/presidents_column/spirituality_work_sept03.htm (Accessed September 1, 2005)

12 www.bartleby.com/65/ec/eclctc-phi.html

5 Seven Essential Traits of a Spiritual Person

THE JEWEL NET OF INDRA

Far away in the heavenly abode of the great god Indra, there is a wonderful net that has been hung by some cunning artificer in such a manner that it stretches out infinitely in all directions. In accordance with the extravagant tastes of deities, the artificer has hung a single glittering jewel in each "eye" of the net, and since the net itself is infinite in all dimensions, the jewels are infinite in number. There hang the jewels, glittering like stars of the first magnitude, a wonderful sight to behold.

If we now arbitrarily select one of these jewels for inspection and look closely at it, we will discover that in its polished surface there are reflected all the other jewels in the net, infinite in number. Not only that, but each of the jewels reflected in this one jewel is also reflecting all the other jewels, so that there is an infinite reflecting process occurring. The Hua-yen school has been fond of this image, mentioned many times in its literature, because it symbolizes a cosmos in which there is an infinitely repeated interrelationship among all the members of the cosmos. This relationship is said to be one of simultaneous mutual identity and mutual intercausality.[1]

Know that the whole world is a mirror. In each atom are found a hundred blazing suns. If you split the center of a single drop of water, A hundred oceans spring forth. . . Everything is brought together at the point of the present.
— Mahmud Shabesteri, 14th Century Islamic Poet

> Spirituality rejoices in the interdependence of all things. In fact, spirituality . . . may be defined as "the art of making connections;" connections not only between individuals, but also between communities and nations. Its *raison d'etre* is for the celebration of unity in unimaginable diversity; of a transcendent meaning that holds all things together and gives us hope; of what the old theologians would have called the divine coinherence.[2]
>
> — Alan Jones

There is no list of attributes that you can examine and check off to prove that you are a spiritual person. The seven characteristics discussed in this chapter are representative, not exhaustive, but in my opinion they are essential.

The first three traits relate to who you are within yourself. These traits form a *Circle of Being: authenticity, integrity, and humility,* with each characteristic dependent on the others. All together they form the foundation of your sense of self and of your sense of place and belonging in the universe.

The last four traits take you out of yourself into the larger community. These traits form a *Circle of Connection: openness, hospitality, gratitude, and compassion,* with each characteristic feeding the others. Together they feed your sense of connectedness to life, the world, other people, and transcendent reality (God/Spirit/Universe).

As you become more and more aware of your belonging and your connectedness, these six characteristics grow in you. Like the Jewel Net of Indra or the World Wide Web of the internet, each of these characteristics affects each of the others.

After we discuss each of the seven traits, we will continue with a section on self-discovery, outlining seven practical steps that you can take to make progress in these areas. The chapter concludes with a peek at what's ahead.

Authenticity

> Authenticity is a secular word for grace.
> – Anthony Padovano

Authenticity is the character trait of being genuine, real, and honest both with yourself and others. An authentic person "walks the talk"—"what-you-see-is-what-you-get." An authentic individual is genuine, not counterfeit.

An *in*authentic person is insincere, deceptive, hypocritical, disingenuous, and phony.

If you are authentic, you are reliable and take responsibility for your own mistakes. You accept responsibility for outcomes in the work done by those under your direction. You know that "the buck stops here."

An authentic person is "a genuine original" who makes up his or her own mind based on inner values. Being authentic means you act on your own authority, based on your own carefully considered values. Authenticity keeps you from being subject to the pressure to be like your peers and the pressure to give up your own sense of self to please others and get ahead.

John Baldoni, a leadership communications consultant, writes:

> Authenticity is not a nice-to-have; it's a leadership imperative . . . . Communications is essential to that conveyance process. Every manager must resonate a degree of authenticity. In simplest terms, it means you stand up for what you believe and you deliver on what you promise. Simple, yes, but challenging to live by.[3]

To be authentic—a genuine original—you must know who you are. The establishment of a personal identity is a crucial task of adolescence, but from then on it is an ongoing task of all human beings. As long as we change and grow, we need to keep rediscovering our inner selves, re-evaluating our values, re-orienting ourselves to fulfill our deepest purpose, and adjusting our actions to match.

Integrity

> The workplace is the litmus test for integrity. There is nothing
> easy about integrating what you believe with how you behave.[4]
> — Sandi Dolbee

Integrity: The Integration of Your Self

Integrity comes from the same root word as *integer,* which refers
to a whole number. As a character trait, integrity refers to your inner unity or wholeness, which is the result of the *integration* of your
self. This integration grows through life-long inner reflection and
growing self-understanding.

Integrity: Being Faithful to Commitments

Integrity[5] also involves "holding steadfastly true" to your commitments. Commitments include promises to yourself or to others,
convictions about right and wrong or about God or faith, and
relationships. Different commitments are at different levels of
importance, and many commitments change over time.

With which commitments in your life do you identify most
deeply? Which commitments best define what your life is really
about? If you are not true to a commitment of this type, the meaning
of your life loses its identity or individuality.

An integrity that includes faithfulness to these commitments
leads you

> to act in a way that accurately reflects your sense of who you
> are; to act from motives, interests and commitments that are
> most deeply your own . . . . If a person fails to act on their core
> commitments, through self-deception, weakness of will,
> cowardice, or even ignorance, then they lack integrity.[6]

If your self-understanding is incomplete or unrealistic, your
commitments may not be true to your real self. Moreover, if your
commitments are harmful to yourself and/or others, you may "act
with integrity" but not be considered a person of integrity.

Integrity: The Social Dimension

Always do right—this will gratify some and astonish the rest.

– Mark Twain

A person of integrity stands for something "within a community of people trying to discover what in life is worth doing."[7] Such a person understands his or her role in the larger community and respects the judgments of others in the community.

Cheshire Calhoun explains that:

Lying about one's views, concealing them, recanting them under pressure, selling them out for rewards or to avoid penalties, and pandering to what one regards as the bad views of others, all indicate a failure to regard one's own judgment as one that should matter to others.[8]

Integrity: Morals and Ethics

Finally, integrity has come to mean *moral or ethical soundness or wholeness* as well as wholeness of one's self—in other words, "the quality or condition of being whole or undivided; completeness."[9]

Humility

Humility is a virtue, not a neurosis.[10]

– Thomas Merton

Humility has a "bad rap" in our society. Sometimes we equate humility with someone who has become a doormat in a bad job or in an abusive relationship. Other times we equate humility with a "poor me" attitude of martyrdom that is put on and worn as a means of manipulating and controlling others. Such a person is not humble.

Humility comes from the Latin word *humus*, meaning *ground*. It is an understanding and acknowledgement of who we *really* are. Humility is an admission of our earthiness, our creatureliness. It means that we don't try to control people or fix situations that are clearly beyond us. We accept our limitations. We don't try to play God.

> One of the symptoms of an approaching nervous breakdown is the belief that one's work is terribly important.
> – Bertrand Russell (1872-1970)

Humility: Being Grounded

Humility means being down-to-earth, not "putting on airs." Being "down to earth" or being "grounded" does not mean being walked on or abased. It does mean that you understand that you are a human being. You have a physical body that consists of the same elements that make up the earth. You need food, and rest, and exercise. Your knowledge and understanding—and also your intelligence—have limitations.

> A spiritual person is one who has the humility that comes from reverence and "an overriding appreciation of awe and mystery."[11]

Humility: Knowing the Truth About Yourself

When you are willing to discover, face, and acknowledge the truth about yourself, you learn that you are much more amazing than you ever dreamed.

Humility requires admitting your human, creature limits and meeting your human, creature needs—but not in self-criticism or self-punishment. Humility does not make you guilt-ridden, but causes you to acknowledge your limitations and admit your needs. It is the humble who know how to ask for help—and get it. If your inner driving need is to be in-dispensable, to be in control, to take all the credit at work, and to look good to others, you probably won't see humility when you look inside yourself.

Humility enables—and requires—that you admit when you are wrong, even to your co-workers, and ask forgiveness.

Humility also requires that you acknowledge your gifts—your particular skills and talents, your unique view of life.

Use what talents you possess: the woods would be very silent if
no birds sang there except those that sang best.
– Henry Van Dyke

Humility requires accepting responsibility while understanding that you are not in control of everything that happens.

Humility requires the courage to listen, hear and follow what you believe is right—even when you feel totally inadequate to the task.

In his book *Run with the Horses*, Eugene Peterson describes Irijah the Sentry, a character in the book of Jeremiah in the Hebrew Scriptures. Irijah was a bureaucrat, and Peterson explains that he was "a person who hides behind the rules and prerogatives of a job description to do work that destroys people."[12]

Adolf Eichmann was another such person. His defense at his trial was that he was merely doing his job when he participated in the killing of six million Jews in Nazi Germany. Peterson explains:

Incalculable evil comes from these unlikely sources: quiet,
efficient, little people doing their job, long since having given
up thinking of themselves as responsible, moral individuals.[13]

In other words, they have no idea of their identity. They have no idea that they can cause such evil—and they certainly have no idea how valuable they can be if they are willing to become who they really are.

Leadership communications consultant John Baldoni writes:

Humility is not taught in management courses or many leadership courses, for that matter. And you can understand why.
Organizations want their leaders to be visionary, authoritative,
capable and motivational. Nowhere does it say anything about
being "humble."

Still, most successful leaders understand that a sense of
humility is essential to winning hearts and minds. Humility is a
visible demonstration of concern and compassion, as well as
authenticity. Leaders who are to be followed must be leaders
who understand the human condition, especially their own.
Those in authority who are blind to their inner selves are likely
to do stupid things, like invade Russia (Napoleon), invade
France and Russia (Hitler) and invade Kuwait (Saddam) . . . .

> Humility is admission of humanity, a sense that leader and follower are in this together. That deepens a sense of trust. Better to admit a shortcoming, or a limitation, than to lead blindly onto the unknown . . . .
>
> Humility is the grace note of leadership.[14]

Humility: Facing Life With a Sense of Humor

> Life is too important to be taken seriously.
>
> – Oscar Wilde

Essential to being a completely human person of humility is the ability to see the absurdity and ridiculousness of things that happen, and the ability to laugh at life and at yourself. You can't do that if you don't have the humility to accept your own failures.

A sense of humor at work enables you to laugh, and to help others laugh, when things that are beyond control go wrong, such as a computer crash or a snowstorm. That doesn't mean you don't work to correct and surmount the problems. It simply means you accept the fact that all your careful plans must now be adapted to the unexpected situation.

Humor must be safe for others. You can poke fun at your own behavior and your own expense; but disparaging others, even in jest, belittles and puts down the other rather than sharing fun and lightening the workload.

Openness

John B. Bennett[15] describes two types of spirituality in academia, which we see in all parts of society. One is "aggressive or insistent individualism." The other is focused on community:

> Alternatively, we may cherish a broader community and look to it to help provide the enduring importance we seek. We sense that we can possess true autonomy only by acknowledging and celebrating our interdependence with others . . . . Practicing openness to a plurality of perspectives upon the world—a

plurality of ideas, values, and concepts of truth, beauty, and goodness—enables us to grow personally and profession-ally . . . .

As we grow in our humanity, we grow in relationship to the good and to responsibility for the good of others. When this happens, we extend our horizons and move from practicing personal openness to embracing the connectivity of the world. Indeed, we move into the fundamental trust that the ultimate nature of reality is itself hospitable—that it provides the primordial model for how we are to live.[16]

Hospitality

Hospitality is openness that is focused on the other person, espe-cially the stranger, who may in fact be someone you have "known" at work for years. The person who is most different from you is the per-son toward whom you can best show hospitality.

To be hospitable, you need to accept pluralism as a natural condition in the world. Celebrate the diversity of the Creation. One particularly valuable spin-off of hospitality is inter-religious dialogue.[17]

Hospitality and *hostility* originate from the same root meaning *stranger* and branching to mean either guest or enemy. *Host* is liter-ally the "lord of strangers." A host may refer to an army as well as to a welcoming person.

Hospitality is essential to spiritual practice. It reminds you that you are part of a greater whole . . . . Putting others first puts you in the midst of life without the illusion of being the center of life.

— Rabbi Rami M. Shapiro[18]

Gratitude

If the only prayer you say in your life is "Thank you," that would be enough.

– Meister Eckhart

Brother David Steindl-Rast, O.S.B., says that "profound grate-fulness is always a sign" of a profound experience that psychologist Abraham Maslow called a "peak experience" and that may also be called a mystical or numinous experience.[19]

He goes on to explain that gratitude enables us to move

> from suspicion to trust, from proud isolation to a humble give and take, from enslavement to false independence to self-acceptance in that dependence which liberates.[20]

Moreover:

> Suspicion will not even recognize a gift as gift: who can prove that it isn't a lure, a bribe, a trap? Gratefulness has the courage to trust and so overcomes fear. . . . You can feel either grateful or alienated, but never both at the same time. . . . When you are grateful you know that you belong to a network of give-and-take and you say "yes" to that belonging.[21]

Compassion

> No one is useless in this world who lightens the burden of it for anyone else.
>
> – Charles Dickens

The word *compassion* comes from words meaning *to suffer together*. Compassion is based on empathy, the ability to feel with another person as though you are that other person.

Tim Sanders, chief solutions officer for Yahoo! and author of *The Likeability Factor* and *Love Is the Killer App,* said the following about compassion:

> It's a very contagious thing . . . . When [psychologist and author Abraham] Maslow carefully pointed out to me that people are good, and when they do bad things it's because they're coping with unfulfilled needs, I was a different manager overnight. I was a different employee overnight. I stopped saying, "buyers are liars," "my boss is a jerk," "the employees

will abuse you." And I said, "So, what is my boss going through?"

It helped me understand.[22]

Compassion goes a step further than empathy. Compassion *suffers with* the other person. Compassion tries to eliminate that suffering but continues to *suffer with* the person if eliminating the suffering is impossible. We learn compassion from our own failures and from knowing and accepting our own woundedness and vulnerabilities. These unpleasant human experiences remind us that we are not God and teach us that we are one with each other.

> A human being is part of a whole, called by us the Universe
> . . . . He experiences himself, his thoughts and feelings, as
> something separated from the rest—a kind of optical delusion of
> his consciousness. This delusion is a kind of prison for us. . .
> Our task must be to free ourselves from this prison by widening
> our circles of compassion to embrace all living creatures and
> the whole of nature in its beauty.
>
> – Albert Einstein

Compassion is an inevitable result of humility and an essential antidote to greed:

> Compassion, we believe, is rooted in three inter-related
> factors: first, a basic rational honesty contained in the under-
> standing that our personal interests are *not* more important
> than the interests of others—we are only one individual, after
> all, whereas other people and animals are numberless. We
> cannot credibly justify subordinating the interests of others to
> the needs of this single self. Second, it is rooted in the ability to
> feel the misery of others as real and important, to not be so
> totally swallowed up by our own goals and desires that we are
> numb to their pain.

> Hidden away alongside this rational honesty and emotional
> sensitivity is another factor promoting compassion—the sense
> that reining-in self-concern and increasing our concern for
> others is also conducive to our own well-being. Focusing solely
> on our own needs places those needs—which are, after all,
> problems—firmly at the centre of our psychological universe.
> Like objects under a magnifying glass, to the extent and

intensity that we focus on these problems, the larger and more important they seem to us.[23]

Discovering Who You Really Are

Quiet time alone is essential to the development of each of these essential traits.

In order to be *authentic*, a genuine original, you must know who you are. The establishment of a personal identity is a crucial task of adolescence, but from then on, it is an ongoing task of all human beings. As long as we change and grow, we need to keep rediscovering our inner selves, re-evaluating our inner values, re-orienting ourselves to fulfill our deepest purpose, and adjusting our actions to match.

Becoming a person of *integrity* also involves a significant investment in personal reflection. How else can you grow into the integration of your personality? How else can you come to understand what your deepest convictions and commitments should be? How else can you learn your role in the community and develop morally and ethically?

Time and reflection are crucial to developing the *humility* that comes from your experience of awe and mystery before God. Inner reflection is necessary to discovering both your limits and your unique gifts.

Openness, hospitality, gratitude, and *compassion* depend on your spending time reviewing your actions and thinking about your own existential situation as well as putting yourself into the situations of others.

The following section suggests concrete steps to help you focus on developing these traits.

Seven Steps in Getting There From Here

These suggestions are intended to supplement, not replace, any individual faith disciplines you already practice, such as daily Bible reading, Buddhist meditation, Islamic prayer or Jewish devotional practice. Spend time in quiet reflection, preferably daily. Listen to your inner being. Here are some suggestions:

1. You may listen best by sitting in silent meditation and contemplation or by taking a quiet walk through nature or by listening to inspiring music.

2. Pay attention to your physical body. What is your body trying to tell you? What is out of synch between you and your environment?

   Does your neck hurt? Who or what is your "pain in the neck?" How can you be your authentic self with this annoying person or situation?

   Is your stomach tied in knots? What is causing fear in your life and how is that fear preventing you from living authentically?

   Do you have a headache? Is it stress? What can you do to avoid, alleviate, or deal with that stress?

3. Keep a record of this daily listening. If you write comfortably, keep a journal as part of our daily routine. No one has to see it but you. Remember to include things you are thankful for every day. Perhaps sketching or painting is a more flowing expression for you—not everything has to be put into words.

4. Review your journal (or art or whatever you do) at least monthly. You will be amazed at the insights you will gain about yourself.

5. Share your life's journey with others beyond your immediate family. You will find that close friends, members of you faith community, or students in a continuing education class are likely to share some of the questions and situations that you yourself face in daily life and work.

6. Start a workplace or community series on Workplace Spirituality. Your group can decide whether to focus on mutual support and discussion, bring in speakers who deal with different aspects of Workplace Spirituality, or study ethical issues.

7. Be willing to seek help. Consult with a physician if you experience signs of agitation or clinical depression or if you experience uncontrollable rage. Talk with a therapist if you need help with personal problems and/or your relationships. Find a spiritual director (sometimes called a spiritual guide or spiritual friend) or a coach to help you listen to God on your spiritual journey.

Looking Ahead

Chapter 6, "Spiritual Behaviors on the Job," lists concrete behaviors at work that should result from each of the spiritual traits described in this chapter. The chapter concludes with specific developmental tasks that are part of this spiritual and behavioral growth process.

Endnotes

1 From the *The Avatamsaka Sutra* in Francis H. Cook, *Hua-Yen Buddhism: The Jewel Net of Indra,* (Pennsylvania State University Press, 1977) p. 2
2 Alan Jones, *Soul Making: The Desert Way of Spirituality* (HarperSanFrancisco, 1985) p. 23-24
3 "It's the Real Thing: Authenticity" by John Baldoni, http://www.darwinmag.com/read/020104/authentic.html February, 2004
4 http://www.signonsandiego.com/news/features/20040422-9999-lz1c22 work.html (Accessed February 28, 2006)
5 I am indebted to the *Stanford Encyclopedia of Philosophy* at http://plato.stanford.edu/entries/integrity/ for a discussion of various understandings of integrity.
6 *Ibid.*
7 *Ibid.*
8 Calhoun, Cheshire (1995). "Standing for Something," *Journal of Philosophy* XCII, pp. 235-260
9 The Free Dictionary, http://www.thefreedictionary.com/integrity (Accessed March 13, 2006)
10 Thomas Merton, *Thoughts in Solitude* Farrar, Straus and Giroux (November 29, 1999)
11 Jones, *op. cit.,* p. 3
12 Eugene Peterson, *Run with the Horses,* (Downers Grove, IL: InterVarsity Press, 1983) p. 162
13 *Ibid.*

14 John Baldoni, "Humility," http://www.darwinmag.com/read/060104/baldoni.html (Accessed October 4, 2005)

15 John B. Bennett is Provost Emeritus and University Scholar at Quinnipiac University in Hamden, CT (john.bennett@quinnipiac.edu). His most recent book is *Academic Life: Hospitality, Ethics, and Spirituality* (Bolton, MA: Anker Publishing, 2003).

16 John B. Bennett, "Academic Spirituality," *Spirituality in Higher Education,* April 2004. http://www.spirituality.ucla.edu/newsletter/past/Volume%20I/1/1.html (Accessed January 7, 2006) The material in this essay reflects themes in a new book manuscript, entitled *The Roles of Spirituality in Academic Life: A Primer.*

17 Adapted from Frederic and Mary Ann Brussat, *Spiritual Rx: Prescriptions for Living a Meaningful Life* (Hyperion, 2000)

18 *Minyan: Ten Principles for Living a Life of Integrity* (Bell Tower, 1997) Spirituality & Health, http://www.spiritualityhealth.com/newsh/items/soulbooster/item_662.html (Accessed January 9, 2006)

19 Brother David Steindl-Rast, O.S.B., "All in the Same Boat," Reprinted from *New Age,* September 1983, Vol. 9, #2, pp. 36-40 and 62-64. http://www.gratefulness.org/readings/dsr_SameBoat4.htm (Accessed January 7, 2006)

20 Steindl-Rast, "A Deep Bow: Gratitude as the root of a common religious language," *Main Currents in Modern Thought* (May-June 1967, Vol. 23, No. 5, pp. 129-132), reprinted on http://www.gratefulness.org/readings/dsr_DeepBow2.htm (Accessed January 4, 2006)

21 Steindl-Rast, "A New Reason for Gratitude" http://www.gratefulness.org/readings/dsr_reason.htm (Accessed January 7, 2006)

22 Quoted by Amanda Paulson, "A 'lovecat' calls for compassion in the cubicles," *The Christian Science Monitor,* March 4, 2002, http://www.csmonitor.com/2002/0304/p17s01-wmwo.html (Accessed February 28, 2006)

23 http://www.medialens.org/alerts/03/030514_Demolishing_Compassion.html (Accessed May 27, 2005)

6 Spiritual Behaviors on the Job

᭮᭮᭮᭮᭮᭮᭮᭮᭮᭮᭮᭮᭮᭮᭮᭮᭮᭮᭮᭮᭮᭮᭮᭮᭮᭮᭮᭮᭮᭮᭮᭮᭮᭮᭮᭮᭮᭮᭮

Many people lead bad lives that would gladly lead good ones, but do not know how to make the change.

- Benjamin Franklin

᭮᭮᭮᭮᭮᭮᭮᭮᭮᭮᭮᭮᭮᭮᭮᭮᭮᭮᭮᭮᭮᭮᭮᭮᭮᭮᭮᭮᭮᭮᭮᭮᭮᭮᭮᭮᭮᭮᭮

Spirituality Expressed in Concrete Behaviors

Tim McGuire is the author of a weekly syndicated column for United Media[1] called "More Than Work," covers ethics, spirituality, and values in work. McGuire brings home the importance of the behavioral requirements of spirituality in the workplace in his column for November 3, 2003:

> Some people who pursue spirituality in their work are comfortable with an abstract approach to the subject. I contend decency must follow spiritual intent. Yellers and screamers, connivers and schemers and mean-spirited haters

are going to struggle to find peace in the workplace, no matter how many silent prayers they utter. I know I did.[2]

McGuire goes a step further to include the mood that we bring to the workplace:

Many of us wish for a chance to do big heroic acts, but we build our legacy with a thousand little acts. If we're going to find the transcendent in our everyday lives, we must take personal responsibility for our mood, our attitude, and for the persona we project.[3]

He urges every worker to develop a personal code for work. The code should reflect your ideals but be concrete enough for you to progress toward it and eventually achieve it.

In this chapter we will explore the behaviors that should result from the seven essential traits of a spiritual person discussed in the previous chapter:

- Authenticity
- Integrity
- Humility
- Openness
- Hospitality
- Gratitude
- Compassion

Finally, the chapter concludes with specific developmental tasks that are part of this spiritual and behavioral growth process.

Authentic Behaviors

If you are an authentic person, you will not only "talk the talk" but you will also "walk the walk." In the words of John Baldoni, "you stand up for what you believe and you deliver on what you promise."[4]

As an authentic person, you will:

1. Communicate clearly and accurately to all with whom you work. Make your expectations very clear to those who report to you. Make your commitments to your own peers and managers very clear as well.

2. Be genuinely yourself, not a phony. Present yourself to your bosses, your co-workers, and your employees as you really are. Do not deceive others to get them to like you or to get ahead competitively.

3. Make your decisions and actions reflect your beliefs and values.

4. Resist peer pressure and act with courage, on your own inner authority, from your own carefully considered values. When you express your opinions, do so modestly and honestly, but without modifying them to please any of your constituent groups.

5. Tell the truth. Be honest, dependable, and reliable in what you say and what you do. Others will know that they can count on you to fulfill your obligations and responsibilities and to keep your word.

6. Take responsibility for your own mistakes. Accept responsibility for outcomes in the work done by those under your direction, knowing that "the buck stops here."

The difference between authenticity and integrity is subtle, but significant. Being an authentic person means discovering and becoming who you really are. It as a life-long movement from accepting yourself, to liking yourself, to actually wanting to *be* yourself.

For example, perhaps you are an extrovert and wish you were more of an introvert. Somewhere along the way, you accept the fact that you are an extrovert. Eventually you come to see the positive aspects of being an extrovert and actually *like* yourself that way. Finally, though you continue to moderate your extroverted behavior appropriately, you live into being an introvert as fully as possible.

Integrated Behaviors

Once you know who you really are, you can integrate your behavior with your core values. As an integrated person—a person of integrity—you will:

1. Keep your word. In the words of Cheshire Calhoun:

   Lying about one's views, concealing them, recanting them under pressure, selling them out for rewards or to avoid penalties, and pandering to what one regards as the bad views of others, all indicate a failure to regard one's own judgment as one that should matter to others.[5]

2. Make realistic commitments at work and keep them. This is important when you set schedules, promise deliverables, and make lists of "gets" and "don't gets" for others on a product or project team.

3. Keep your commitments to your spouse, your family, your God, and to yourself. This may include commitments to sexual and emotional faithfulness to your spouse, to investing time with your children, to spending time with an aging parent, to daily exercise, to daily meditation, to regular prayer and worship in whatever form you accept.

4. Remember that integrity has a social dimension. Make sure that you consider the impact of all your moral and ethical decisions on your community, our society, and our world—including both the earth and all the earth's peoples.

   Do the decisions that you and your company make and the actions you take exploit natural resources? Do they exploit the poor in our country or the poor in other countries? Do they make profit for the company by harming the earth or its peoples?

5. Always act in a moral and ethical way. In the words of Dolbee, "The workplace is the litmus text for integrity." [6]

Humble Behaviors

If you are a person of humility, you know and admit your proper place in life and at work. You are grounded. As you increasingly come to understand that you cannot control other people, you will be able to accept your limitations. In living humbly at work you:

1. Relate to others as an equal. This includes both those who report to you and those who are above you. Humility enables you to know and accept your proper place as a gifted and talented person with much to contribute at work. Humility also teaches you that you don't have all the answers and can learn from others. As Baldoni said, "Humility is admission of humanity, a sense that leader and follower are in this together." [7]

2. Take care of your body in terms of food, rest, exercise, and taking sick time when you are ill. Humility teaches you that you are not indispensable and that it is inconsiderate to share your germs with your coworkers.

3. Pay attention by observing and really listening to all your coworkers.

4. Pay attention also to your inner values, to the needs of the world outside, and to your inner calling.

5. Because you recognize that there are limits to your knowledge and understanding and also to your intelligence, ask for information and advice from others. Appreciate the responses you are given, and accept their sharing graciously and thank those who give it to you.

6. Because you recognize that there are limits to your time and energy, ask for help from others who might also be able to do something that you can do. Appreciate and accept that help, and thank those who give it to you.

7. Accept responsibility. Humility teaches you that you are not in control of everything that happens, even in your chain of responsibility at work. Humility requires that you accept responsibility anyway, both for your own failures and for those in any group you supervise or manage.

8. Act with courage to listen, hear, and do what you believe is right—even when you feel totally inadequate to the task. Humility requires you to accept responsibility for your actions when you are ordered to do something that goes against your own values.

9. Take your work seriously, but take yourself lightly. Maintaining your sense of humor builds trust and confidence among your co-workers.

As a humble, authentic person, you make your own decisions, act with integrity, and accept the consequences of your decisions and your actions. This proves you are a person of integrity. Remember that "incalculable evil comes from . . . quiet, efficient, little people doing their job, long since having given up thinking of themselves as responsible, moral individuals."[8]

Open Behaviors

If you are truly open and receptive to others, your behavior exhibits respect for others. You:

1. Are open with information at work, not holding it closely in order to have an advantage over others.

2. Always treat others with respect.

3. Listen attentively and truly hear what others have to say. Those "others" include everyone in your group and the lowest person in the company organization, as well as the CEO. Listen with an expectancy that every speaker has something from which you can learn. Remember that "practicing openness to a plurality of perspectives . . . enables us to grow personally and professionally." [9]

4. Keep confidences.

Hospitable Behaviors

Extending hospitality is a matter of extending openness to include those who are strangers to you, those who are different from you in any way, and those who need your welcome and/or your help.

> When individuals and institutions commit to practicing hospitality, fragmentation and isolation are left behind. The procedural openness to others with which we start is transformed into an openness of being.[10]

As a hospitable person, you:

1. Initiate a welcome invitation toward those you don't know, especially those who are different from you and whose difference makes you feel uncomfortable. As Rabbi Shapiro reminds us:

   > Hospitality is essential to spiritual practice. It reminds you that you are part of a greater whole . . . . Putting others first puts you in the midst of life without the illusion of being the center of life.[11]

2. Put the other person's needs and comfort ahead of your own.

3. Demonstrate a willingness to set aside your work to receive, listen to, and assist the other person, even if that means you must make up your work on your own time.

4. Serve and help the other person.

Grateful Behaviors

As a grateful person, you:

1. Express appreciation to others and to their managers for the things they do for you personally. Steindl-Rast reminds us that we "can feel either grateful or alienated, but never both at the same time. . . . When you are grateful you know that you belong to a network of give-and-take and you say "yes" to that belonging."[12]

2. Express appreciation to others and to their managers for the work they are doing for the business.

3. Look for, affirm, and recognize the contributions that others make to the business and to others in the workplace.

4. Look for, affirm, and recognize the value of other specific individuals in the workplace.

Compassionate Behaviors

Compassionate behavior is based on empathy, the ability to feel with another person as though you are that other person. Contrary to the competitive "I win, you lose" model of business that some accept, empathy and compassion definitely *are* appropriate to the workplace. But much in our culture attempts to eliminate compassion:

> Mainstream culture has a vested interest in suppressing compassion for people and animals beyond our immediate circle of family and friends. The point is that self-seeking greed and compassion are opposed. Vested interests, such as advertisers, want us locked into desire mode, thinking primarily of ourselves, working hard to earn, buy and consume. The last thing our profit-maximising system wants is teenagers concorned about civilian victims of bombing in Iraq, or tortured animals in our farming system. Compassion, therefore, has to be ridiculed as "naïve" and "sentimental."[13]

As a compassionate person, you:

1. Keep communication clear.

2. Cooperate and collaborate with others in their goals and their methods.

3. Practice empathic understanding by intentionally putting yourself in the other person's shoes.

4. Show your genuine concern for others through acts of kindness.

5. Serve others.

Spiritual Behaviors in the World's Great Religions

As part of the whole universe, you learn compassion as you discover the unity of the human condition. This compassion for others is expressed in behaviors that follow the "Golden Rule" of the world's great religions:

Judaism

What is hateful to you, do not to your fellow men. That is the entire Law; all the rest is commentary.

—Talmud, Shabbat, 31a

Hinduism

This is the sum of duty: Do naught unto others which would cause you pain if done to you.

— Mahabharata, 5:1517

Buddhism

Hurt not others in ways that you yourself would find hurtful.

— Udana-Varga 5:18

Confucianism

Surely it is the maxim of loving-kindness: Do not unto others that you would not have them do unto you.

— Analects 15:23

Taoism

Regard your neighbor's gain as your own gain, and your neighbor's loss as your own loss.

— T'ai Shang Kan Ying P'ien

Christianity

All things whatsoever ye would that men should do to you, do ye even so to them: for this is the Law and the Prophets.

— Matthew 7:12

Islam

No one of you is a believer until he desires for his brother that which he desires for himself.

— Sunnah

Seven Developmental Tasks for Spiritual Growth

Becoming who you really are as a person of authenticity, integrity and humility is a life-long process. Learning to demonstrate openness, hospitality, gratitude, and compassion in the workplace is neither quick nor automatic.

The continual, on-going personal spiritual work you must do to grow in these behaviors includes the following seven developmental tasks:

1. Spend some time each day reflecting on your day. Here a simplified version of the *examen of consciousness,* can be useful. The *examen of consciousness* is a spiritual exercise originating with St. Ignatius of Loyola, founder of the Jesuits. If you are new to this kind of daily reflection, focus on two simple questions for your reflection: (1) When was I most alive today (or when did I feel closest to God or when did I feel most like my real self)? (2) When was I least alive today (or when did I feel farthest from God or the least like my real self)?

2. Develop an attitude of openness to new self-discoveries. Do the inner personal work to develop your self-understanding and to make commitments that are not harmful to yourself or others. For example, a commitment to work 70 hours a week, especially over an extended period of time, is likely to be harmful to your own health as well as to your family relationships.

3. Frequently re-evaluate and affirm or change your core inner values.

4. Re-orient yourself to fulfill your deepest purpose as it unfolds.

5. Participate in a community of faith or of seekers or in some kind of community that takes seriously both introspection and social issues.

6. Adjust all your actions to match the new insights you gain.

7. The next day, begin again. . . .

Looking Ahead

Chapter 7, "Ethical Elements in Business," begins Part III of this book: "The Ethics of Working It All Out." Chapter 7 discusses the differences between a vision, values, and ethical principles and why it is important for a business to have each of these. The chapter also provides examples of some specific companies that have been recognized for their ethical business practices, and then contrasts the failures of Enron with the personal spiritual characteristics discussed in Chapters 5 and 6.

Endnotes

1   Copyright 2005, More than Work Distributed by United Feature Syndicate, Inc.
2   *Ibid.*
3   *Ibid.*
4   "It's the Real Thing: Authenticity" by John Baldoni, *Darwin Online,* http://www.darwinmag.com/read/020104/authentic.html February, 2004
5   Calhoun, Cheshire (1995), "Standing for Something," *Journal of Philosophy* XCII, pp. 235-260
6   http://www.signonsandiego.com/news/features/20040422-9999-lz1c22 work.html
7   "Humility" from his column "On Leadership Communications," *Darwin Online* http://www.darwinmag.com/read/060104/baldoni.html (Accessed October 4, 2005)
8   Peterson, *op. cit.*
9   Bennett, *op. cit.*
10 *Ibid.*
11 Rabbi Rami M. Shapiro, *Minyan: Ten Principles for Living a Life of Integrity* (Bell Tower, 1997) Spirituality & Health, http://www.spiritualityhealth.com/newsh/items/soulbooster/item_662.html (Accessed January 9, 2006)·
12 Steindl-Rast, "A New Reason for Gratitude" http://www.gratefulness.org/readings/dsr_reason.htm (Accessed January 7, 2006)
13 http://www.medialens.org/alerts/03/030514_Demolishing_ Compassion.html (Accessed May 27, 2005)

Part III   The Ethics of Working It All Out

In Chapters 7-10, you will think through:

Indispensable elements of an ethical business

Issues and debates in Corporate Social Responsibility

Changing theories on the role of business

Global Perspectives

Examples of award-winning companies

7   Ethical Elements in Business

THE YOUNG BOY AND THE SNAKE

As young boys, Native Americans are often sent away in search of a vision. As one particular boy was climbing to the top of the mountain in search of his vision, he felt the air getting cooler and cooler.

The boy came upon a snake lying in the path. The snake was shivering, and said to the boy, "Please help me. . . I can't move. I need to go down the mountain, but I am so cold that I cannot make it any further."

The young boy said to the snake, "No way! You're a snake. If I pick you up, you'll bite me!"

The snake replied, "No, no. I won't! I promise I won't bite you if you'll only pick me up and help get me down the mountain." So the boy picked up the snake, put him in his shirt, and continued climbing to the top of the mountain in search of his vision.

When the boy returned to the bottom of the mountain after his vision quest, he reached into his shirt and took out the snake. The snake promptly bit him!

The boy said to the snake "Hey! You bit me! You said that if I'd help you out, you wouldn't bite me!" The snake replied to the boy, "But you knew what I was when you picked me up!"

ᘓᘓᘓᘓᘓᘓᘓᘓᘓᘓᘓᘓᘓᘓᘓᘓᘓᘓᘓᘓᘓᘓᘓᘓᘓᘓᘓᘓᘓᘓᘓᘓᘓᘓᘓ

This chapter describes the business elements that determine the ethics of the company. If you put the wrong values first, the snake you carry next to your heart will turn on you and bite you:

- If you put profit first, it can easily become the snake that will fatten itself on human, community, and ecological values; then it will turn and devour you.

- If you put competition first, you will have difficulty finding room for ethics.

- If you put stock prices first, you will have trouble maintaining quality.

In this chapter we will explore the needs of a business to have a vision, values, and ethical principles. You can find many resources to help you and your company develop, articulate, and communicate your vision, values, and ethical principles but here the emphasis is on understanding what these elements are and why they are important.

Next, we will look at examples of some specific companies that have received awards for their excellence in some aspect of business ethics.

Finally, we will contrast a high-level view of the failures of Enron with the personal spiritual characteristics discussed in Chapters 5 and 6, point out how the general public differs with business leaders in their views of ethics, and end the chapter with some questions for your reflection.

Vision

The crux of the matter, I believe, comes down to the purpose of business. So long as companies continue to unapologetically claim that the primary purpose of business is to increase shareholder value, the public will always distrust them. . . . Financial returns are the means to an end, not the end itself.[1]
– Wayne Visser

We have moved from a time when a company goal was to produce *a needed product* or service to an emphasis on *creating a desire* and convincing customers that it is a need.

We've moved from a company goal of contributing to society to make life better for everyone, to a consumer culture that defines people—and causes us to define ourselves—by the stuff we buy.

We've moved from corporations investing their profits to create better products and services to meet real needs, to making profit for the stockholders and building a wealthy class, with both the goal and the process divorced from ethics as well as from spirituality.

> Your vision will become clear only when you look into your heart. . . Who looks outside, dreams. Who looks inside, awakens.
>
> – Carl Jung

Does your company have a meaningful vision statement? What is the big picture? What is your company's reason for existing? Without a vision, the people, the employees, the managers, and the company will perish.[2]

> Leadership begins with a clear vision. There are two aspects of leadership—a visionary role (doing the right thing) and an implementation role (doing things right). A vision is a picture of the future that produces passion and it's this passion that I and other people want to follow. An organization without clear vision is like a river without banks—it stagnates and goes nowhere.[3]

You may have become a manager because you have been able to do things right and you are skilled at leading others in doing the business of your company in the right way. But it takes a real leader to inspire workers to do the right thing.

Your corporate vision should be short, easy to remember and inspiring. It should present a picture of what your company wants to be and to achieve. Because it is future-oriented, it can be broad, but it is most useful if it is specific enough to present a word picture. After all, *vision* is something you can somehow *see* in your mind's eye. It is a group of words that calls up an image.

A vision does not include methods or instructions for how to achieve it. In fact, in Biblical descriptions of visions, the person who sees and is inspired by the vision often asks, "How can this be?" or "How can this happen?"

> Why are we here? Many people assume, wrongly, that a company exists solely to make money. People get together and exist as a company so that they are able to accomplish something collectively that they could not accomplish separately—they make a contribution to society.
> – David Packard, Co-founder of Hewlett-Packard™ Company

A spiritual workplace must have an authentic vision of integrity (doing the right thing) that inspires the employees. Senior management should be the visionaries and be able to communicate the corporate vision in dramatic and persuasive ways to the employees. Those who originate and communicate the vision must themselves be dedicated to it. To present a highly ethical vision with no accountability at the senior level is to betray everything that is meant by being a spiritual workplace.

What if you are a middle manager in a corporation that lacks a vision or merely gives lip-service to it? Create a vision with and for your group. As a middle manager, you have one of the most difficult tasks in a corporation, for you are "sandwiched" between senior managers and those who perform most of the production or service work of the company.

In his book *The Presidential Difference: Leadership Style from FDR to George W. Bush*, Fred I. Greenstein uses six criteria, including vision, to compare twelve modern presidents. He writes:

> "Vision" is a term with a variety of connotations. One is the capacity to inspire. . . . "Vision" refers to preoccupation with the content of policies, an ability to assess their feasibility, and the possession of a set of overarching goals. . . . Vision also encompasses consistency of viewpoint. Presidents who stand firm are able to set the terms of policy discourse. In effect they serve as anchors for the rest of the political community.

> George H. W. Bush was not alone in lacking "the vision thing." He falls in a class of presidential pragmatists that includes the bulk of the modern chief executives. **The costs of vision-free**

leadership include internally inconsistent programs, policies that have unintended consequences, and sheer drift.[4] [emphasis added]

Caution: A vision is not the same as a mission statement. A mission statement is more concrete. Though a mission statement should also be short and concise, it consists of the company's (or the work group's) goals and priorities. The goals are concrete, realistic, and specific. They may be tied to time periods. You need a mission statement, too, but do not write a mission statement when you intend to write a vision statement.

Values

[Values are] fundamental beliefs that drive organizational behavior and decision making.[5]

A spiritual company thinks through, articulates, and publishes its values. Values define what the company ought to be. Values are the beliefs and principles that express the understanding of the company or group regarding which goals are good or bad and which actions are right or wrong. Corporate values guide managers and all employees in making decisions about acceptable behavior and ethical business decisions.

Robert Fraser, recipient of the Midwest Region Ernst & Young Entrepreneur of the Year Award in 2000, defines the difference between the *entrepreneurial* spirit and the *exploitational* spirit:

Many people believe entrepreneurs are greed-motivated, but that is patently untrue. The most successful entrepreneurs are not driven by greed but by passion for finding and solving the greatest needs. When I teach classes on entrepreneurialism I am often asked how to find a great moneymaking idea. I put it like this: "Find the most people in the most pain, and solve their problem." The essence of the entrepreneurial spirit is meeting others' needs.

The opposite of the entrepreneurial spirit is the exploitational spirit which is more concerned with getting money from a customer (or congregation member) than providing value.

> People (or businesses or churches) with the exploitational spirit pursue riches by using a customer to enrich themselves, instead of serving the customer. . . .
>
> What I call the "sanctity of business" is this:
>
> Business is primarily about serving others, creating value, constantly improving products and services, committing to customers, being there for customers and supporting them long-term. It cannot be successful without intense passion and focus.
>
> The exploitational spirit, on the other hand, tries to make as much money as possible and give as little as possible in return.[6]

Are your company's values aimed at serving others and creating value or are they aimed at making as much money as possible?

If you are a middle manager and your company does not already have a written statement of values, you may want to invite the members of your group to discuss the personal values that are most important to them. They probably have determined their values based on their spirituality or faith. By inviting them to share what their most cherished personal values are *and why*, you are inviting them to "bring their spirituality to work."

Your invitation should not promise too much. You are not asking them to participate in the actual formulation or writing of corporate values. Those values should be coming from the top of the corporation. If your company is small enough and if one of your corporate values is to encourage participation by all, then let them know that. Whichever is the case, be honest.

But you can invite their comments even if you also tell them that corporate values are ultimately formulated by senior management. Such a discussion within your group will help all of you grow in understanding and respect for each other and thus build cohesiveness.

> [Values are those] things (e.g. behaviors, customs, feelings) an organization or its people hold dear and see as necessary to accomplish their vision, and wish to maintain into the future.[7]

Values make up part of the bridge that links your corporate vision, mission, and daily operations. Hudson Associates Consulting, Inc. explains the relationship:

> *Values:* Set of beliefs or standards that the organization (i.e., organizational values) and its stakeholders (i.e., personal values) believe in and operate from. Organizational values are utilized to guide the day-to-day operations, serving as a linkage between Mission (i.e., present operations) and Vision (i.e., intended direction). Personal values are utilized to allow organizational members to understand how their own beliefs fit into the organizational values and its intended operations and direction.[8]

Your stated corporate values provide the information needed for your employees and all your constituents to determine to what extent they share those values. This information will help them know how and where they fit into the corporation and its business. They will also understand that if they do *not* share the corporate values, perhaps they need to consider moving to a different company.

> Shared values are what engender trust and link an organization together. Shared values are also the identity by which an organization is known throughout its business areas. These values must be stated as both corporate objectives and individual values. Every organization and every leader will have a different set of values that are appropriate to its business situation.[9]

Ethical Principles

In his article "Center on Principles," Stephen R. Covey describes a significant difference between principles and values:

> You may think that it's just a matter of semantics and that when most people talk about values they really mean these universal principles. But I see a clear difference between principles and values. Hitler was value-driven; Saddam Hussein is value-driven. Every person and organization is driven by what they value. But they aren't necessarily ethical or principle-centered.[10]

A further examination of these terms supports Covey's distinction. Not all corporate values are ethical values. For example, a company might value profit above everything else, regardless of how its way of doing business affects its employees, customers, competitors, or the world community. *Ethics* are *basic principles* that state or describe right and wrong or good and bad.

> *Principles* are simple, direct statements of an organization's basic beliefs.[11]

> [They are] a set of norms and values that represent what is desirable and positive for an individual, group, organisation or local community and therefore affect the "rightness and wrongness" of actions.[12]

A code of ethics is a set of rules that a company or professional group is expected to follow. The rules may include obligations that employees or members have toward various constituencies. It often includes an introduction stating ideals to which the company or professional group aspires.

> Companies with strong mission, vision and values have an advantage in achieving key business goals. In the landmark 1995 book *Built to Last*, Collins and Porras' analysis of 18 "visionary" companies—companies driven by principles and goals beyond profit maximization—found these businesses achieved growth in shareholder return 12 times that of the general market between 1926 and 1990. More recent studies show correlations between a company's mission, vision and values and its financial performance, customer loyalty and effective risk management.[13]

Growth and Profitability

Non-religious and for-profit companies can be spiritual. Some of the companies described in this chapter have increased their profits since focusing on spiritual values, especially as those values relate to their employees. Putting shareholders first during the past two decades has resulted in poor business, and even worse, unethical and illegal behavior by many companies.

Bill George, former Medtronic® Chairman and CEO, and author of *Authentic Leadership,* led Medtronic's market capitalization from $1.1 billion to $60 billion, averaging 35% a year, under his principle that "shareholders come third." He writes:

> Companies that put their customers first and empower their employees to serve them will inevitably provide greater growth and shareholder value than those corporations that focus primarily on getting their stock price up and only give lip service to the other constituencies.[14]

Moreover, the Executive Summary of the 2003 Report on Socially Responsible Investing Trends in the United States says:

> Socially and environmentally responsible investing in the United States has proven remarkably robust during 2001 and 2002 despite sluggish market conditions that have resulted in a downturn in assets in the wider investment universe. Most notably, socially screened portfolios counted by this Report grew seven percent, while the broader universe of professionally managed portfolios fell four percent.[15]

Companies Recognized for Their Business Ethics

More and more organizations are recognizing companies and leaders that the organization believes exemplify the best practices in business ethics. The following companies received awards from the Business Civic Leadership Center and from *Business Ethics* for excellence in various areas of business ethics.[16] The award criteria used by the groups that honored these companies are listed in Appendix A.

Seventh Generation®, University Bank, and Office Depot®

The United States Chamber of Commerce 2004 Corporate Stewardship Awards given to small, mid-sized, and large companies went to the following businesses:

- **Seventh Generation** [in Vermont] which fosters positive social and environmental change through innovations in producing paper, household cleaning, and baby diaper/wipe products using natural ingredients. The corporate name comes from the Iroquois belief that *"in our every deliberation, we must consider the impact of our decisions on the next seven generations."*

- **University Bank in Minnesota** for developing "inventive products and services that serve economically disadvantaged communities."

- **Office Depot**, "the world's leading retailer of recycled paper products for their environmental and education programs."[17]

When the Chamber set up these awards, it described the Corporate Stewardship Award as follows:

> Corporate stewardship reflects a philosophy that emphasizes the proper use and allocation of a company's resources and unites its ethical values and economic mission. As such, the Corporate Stewardship Award rewards companies for their total performance and contribution to economic, community and social progress.[18]

Clif Bar Inc.

Clif Bar Inc. of Berkeley, California is the winner of the 16th Annual Business Ethics Awards' 2004 General Excellence Award "for its thorough-going commitment to environmental sustainability, employee well-being, and community involvement."[19]

Gary Erickson started the business in his kitchen with $1,000 and was eventually offered $120 million for it in 2000. When he considered that the buy-out would mean the company would be moved and all its employees would be out of work, he reconsidered. To do that he would have to betray his own vision and values.

In spite of competition from giants like Nestle® and Kraft®, Clif Bar is worth $100 million today, has several new products, and has been considered one of the fastest-growing private companies in the United States for several years.[20]

3M™ Company

3M, based in St. Paul, Minnesota was the winner of the 15th Annual Business Ethics Awards' 2003 Environmental Excellence Award

> for sustained commitment, innovation, and substantial impact
> in three decades of environmental stewardship. Well-known for
> its waste reduction forays in the mid-70s, 3M is celebrated now
> by Business Ethics for sustaining its commitment over many
> decades—and for taking it into innovative new areas like design
> for environment, which means designing products to walk more
> lightly on the earth.[21]

Making the Spiritual-Ethical Connection

> Before you can inspire with emotion, you must be swamped
> with it yourself. Before you can move their tears, your own
> must flow. To convince them, you must yourself believe.
> – Winston Churchill

The Failure of Enron

In *Fortune's* list of America's Most-Admired Companies in 2000, Enron's management quality rating was in the top three, above that of Cisco Systems® and The General Electric™ Company.[22] By December of that year, Enron declared bankruptcy. Enron's managers quickly came to represent the "dark side" of leadership.

Manfred Kets de Vries[23] identified one such "shadow" characteristic as "mirroring," which is the human tendency to see ourselves the way others see us. Ed Konczal explains that when people around a leader flatter and try to please the leader, the risk is that the leader begins to believe that he or she is the kind of powerful person presented in the words and deeds of those followers. This perception can have disastrous consequences for the organization.[24]

Perhaps a brief overview of Enron's story can help us understand the potential role of spirituality in the workplace. Stephen D. Potts, Chairman of the Board of The Ethics Resource Center[25] and former

Director of the Office of Government Ethics (OGE), describes the discrepancy between values and behavior at Enron:

> The Enron debacle provides a prime example of the pitfalls of having an ethics program on paper but not giving it leadership support. Enron's key four values were touted as the foundational basis for the economic success and prosperity that propelled Enron's profit margins and prompted investors to buy its shares. A flimsy adherence to these values, turning into blatant disregard by Enron's leaders and board, caused the company's self-destruction. Respect, integrity, communication and excellence were just words on paper. The reality of the corporate culture that existed prior to the company's fall was a disregard of these values, as dramatically demonstrated by Enron's board voting to "set aside" its code of ethics, to permit the formation of off the books partnerships by officers of the company. . . . From the top down, leaders in the organization must respect and model the ethics process. When made a part of the organizational culture, good ethics programs will help prevent problems before they occur and resolve issues when they arise. [26]

Enron's four key values spelled out the acronym RICE: Respect, Integrity, Communication, and Excellence.

> **Respect:** We treat others as we would like to be treated ourselves. We do not tolerate abusive or disrespectful treatment. Ruthlessness, callousness and arrogance don't belong here.

> **Integrity:** We work with customers and prospects openly, honestly and sincerely. When we say we will do something, we will do it; when we say we cannot or will not do something, then we won't do it.

> **Communication:** We have an obligation to communicate. Here, we take the time to talk with one another. . . and to listen. We believe that information is meant to move and that information moves people.

> **Excellence:** We are satisfied with nothing less than the very best in everything we do. We will continue to raise the bar for everyone. The great fun here will be for all of us to discover just how good we can really be. [27]

It is easy to become enamored of your own position and impor-tance—in other words, to believe your own press. You need the spiri-tual traits discussed in Chapter 5 to resist and overcome such temp-tations. Ed Konczal highlights these traits in his analysis of compa-nies like Enron in his article "Integrity—The New Leadership Style":

> We've seen too many leaders who lack Integrity. While most companies are not ethically (and now financially) bankrupt like Enron, there still exist leaders whose credibility is in question. Lack of Integrity must not be tolerated since they will undermine everything else that contributes to corporate success. . . .
>
> What employees want most from their business leaders are basic principles integrity, ethics and caring, according to the results of a survey conducted by Right Management Consultants.
>
> Authentic people know their deepest values without hesitation and fulfill them in thought, word and deed. Integrity is their nature. They do not depend on their position for power.[28]

Harvard Business School professor Malcolm S. Salter[29] refers to "ethical drift," which cannot be solved or prevented by new rules. He lists such factors as "an extreme performance-oriented culture," an end-justifies-the-means mentality, "gross incompetence," and collu-sion, which together led eventually to fraud. A focus on performance and success seduced the company into believing in its own excel-lence. [30]

Business Ethics and the General Public

According to a study done for the Kettering Foundation by Public Agenda, the American public and business leaders do not see eye-to-eye on business ethics:

> For [members of the public in the study's] focus groups, the most egregious violators of business ethics were corrupt executives who protected their own wealth while driving their companies to bankruptcy and forcing employees out of jobs. . . .

Both the business leaders and the ordinary Americans we interviewed for this research consistently pointed to basic greed and a general erosion of ethics and morals in society as the principal cause of recent business scandals. But business leaders also talked about the tremendous pressure they were under to show profits, which some said could lead the "ethically vulnerable" to take questionable short-cuts. . . .

Business leaders did not talk about saving jobs in moral and ethical tones the way the public did. According to many of the leaders we spoke with, a CEO's primary responsibility was to shareholders, and layoffs were simply seen as an inevitable part of doing business. . . . They were more sensitive than the public to the limits on a CEO's ability to control day-to-day company operations.

Compared to business leaders, people in the focus groups tended to have a broader definition of what ethical business practices meant. For example, they believed protecting workers from layoffs was a crucial moral consideration. Virtually no business person we interviewed framed layoffs as a moral issue.[31]

Questions for Reflection

1. What are the factors you can think of that could lead a creative, innovative leader into "ethical drift"?

2. Do you believe the essential traits of a spiritual person described in Chapter 5 and the resulting behaviors described in Chapter 6 would prevent ethical misbehavior? Why or why not?

3. How does the story of the young boy and the snake relate to the topic of business ethics?

4. Who should model the vision of a corporation? Who should set the values for a workplace? Who should enforce the ethical principles?

5. What are the roles of senior management, middle management, and other employees?

6. If you are a middle manager in a company whose senior executives either have no stated vision, values, and ethical principles, or ignore them, what should you do?

Looking Ahead

Chapter 8, "The Changing Role of Business," explores some of the underlying theories or reasons for the ethical principles and decisions of businesses. Because many of us have never had a reason to study or consider these foundations, we may wonder why ethical decision-making at the corporate level is so difficult. Just as your spirituality is a foundation of your individual choices, decisions and actions, so the theories about economics and business form the foundation of business ethics.

Endnotes

1   Wayne Visser, "Five Corporate Sustainability Challenges that Remain Unmet" http://www.waynevisser.com/5Schallenges.htm, originally published by *Ethical Corporation,* Issue 31, pp 48-51, July 2004. Based on the presentation "The Journey to Sustainability: True Signals Amidst the Noise," *World Business Academy* Global Mind Change Forum, 2004
2   Proverbs 29:18a (KJV)
3   Ken Blanchard, Bill Hybels, and Phil Hodges, *Leadership by the Book: Tools to Transform Your Workplace* (NY:William Morrow and Company, Inc., 1999), Chapter 17.
4   Fred I. Greenstein, "The Qualities that Bear on Presidential Performance," http://www.pbs.org/wgbh/pages/frontline/shows/choice2004/leadership/greenstein.html (Accessed December 4, 2004)
5   www.asq.org/info/glossary/v.html (Accessed December 6, 2004)
6   Bob Fraser, "What to Love about Money," *Marketplace Christianity,* International Coalition of Workplace Ministries, http://www.icwm.net/articles_view.asp?articleid=6152&columnid (Accessed January 14, 2005)
7   www.patech.com/glossary.htm (Accessed December 6, 2004)
8   http://www.hacinc.com/hacinc/DrDan/glossary/u-v.html (Accessed December 6, 2004)
9   http://www.1000ventures.com/business_guide/crosscuttings/shared_values.html (Accessed December 6, 2004)
10 Stephen R. Covey, "Center on Principles," http://www.franklincovey.com/ez/library/cop.html (Accessed December 6, 2004)

11 http://www.seanet.com/~daveg/glossary.htm Virtual Organization Glossary of Terms (Accessed November 29, 2004)
12 http://www.local.gov.za/DCD/idpmanual/idp07.html (Accessed January 3, 2005)
13 "Mission, Vision, Values," Business for Social Responsibility, http://www.bsr.org/AdvisoryServices/MVV.cfm (Accessed January 12, 2005)
14 Cecil Johnson, "Ex-CEO says concentrating on business, not the stockholders, really does pay," Fort Worth Star-Telegram, Authentic Leadership, http://www.authenticleaders.org/articles/fortworthstar.htm (Accessed May 23, 2005)
15 Social Investment Forum, *2003 Report on Socially Responsible Investing Trends in the United States*, http://www.socialinvest.org/areas/research/trends/sri_trends_report_2003.pdf, p. 4 (Accessed May 23, 2005)
16 *Business Ethics* is a Minneapolis-based, 16-year-old publication focused on corporate social responsibility. For the complete awards story, including criteria, judges, and past winners, see http://www.business-ethics.com/annual.htm (Accessed January 11, 2005)
17 "U.S. Chamber Presents Corporate Citizenship Awards," December 3, 2004, U.S. Chamber of Commerce, http://www.uschamber.com/press/releases/2004/december/04-157.htm (Accessed January 11, 2005)
18 http://www.commerce.gov/opa/press/Secretary_Evans/2003_Releases/June/18_Evans_CorpStewardAward.htm (Accessed July 19, 2005)
19 *Business Ethics* is a Minneapolis-based, 16-year-old publication focused on corporate social responsibility. For the complete awards story, including criteria, judges, and past winners, see http://www.business-ethics.com/annual.htm (Accessed January 11, 2005)
20 For other innovative approaches to ethics on the part of this company, see the company website at http://www.clifbar.com/connect/press.cfm?location=press.
21 Peter Asmus, "15th Annual Business Ethics Awards," http://www.business-ethics.com/15th_annual_business_ethics_awards.htm (Accessed January 11, 2005)
22 Todd N. Lebor, "Most Admired Rule Makers," February 8, 2001, *The Motley Fool,* http://www.fool.com/Server/FoolPrint.asp?File=/portfolios/rulemaker/2001/rulemaker010208.htm (Accessed January 29, 2005)
23 Raoul de Vitry d'Avaucourt Chaired Professor of Leadership Development Clinical Professor of Management and Leadership, INSEAD, Fontainebleau, France
24 Ed Konczal, "Integrity – The New Leadership Story – Part 1," *weLEAD* Online Magazine, http://www.leadingtoday.org/Onmag/june04/ek-june04.html (Accessed January 14, 2005)
25 The Ethics Resource Center (ERC) is a nonprofit, nonpartisan educational organization whose **vision** is a world where individuals and organizations act with integrity. The **mission** of the Ethics Resource Center is to strengthen ethical leadership worldwide by providing leading-edge expertise and services through research, education and partnerships.

26 Stephen D. Potts, "A Case Study of Private-to-Private Corruption," The Ethics Resource Center (ERC), 2003-05, http://www.ethics.org/resources/article_detail.cfm?ID=822 (Accessed January 14, 2005)

27 Enron's "Statement of Human Rights Principles," http://www.enron.com/corp/pressroom/responsibility/human_rights_statement.html (Accessed December 31, 2005)

28 Ed Konczal, "Integrity – The New Leadership Story – Part 2," *weLEAD* Online Magazine, http://www.leadingtoday.org/Onmag/july04/ek-july04.html (Accessed January 14, 2005) This essay was quoted from Chapter 1 of Ed Konczal and Jeannette C. Galvanek, *Simple Stories for Leadership: Insight in the New Economy (*University Press of America, 2005)

29 Malcolm S. Salter is the James J. Hill Professor of Business Administration at Harvard Business School. He has been a member of the faculty since 1967. His teaching and research focus on issues of corporate strategy, organization, and governance.

30 Martha Lagace, "Enron's Lessons for Managers," July 12, 2004, Harvard Business School Working Knowledge, http://hbswk.hbs.edu/pubitem.jhtml?id=4253&t=organizations (Accessed February 28, 2006)

31 *A Few Bad Apples?: An Exploratory Look at What Typical Americans Think about Business Ethics Today,* A Report for the Kettering Foundation from Public Agenda by Steve Farkas, Ann Duffett and Jean Johnson with Beth Syat (January, 2004) p. 2-4

8 The Changing Role of Business

TWO WOLVES

An old Cherokee told his granddaughter about a fight that was going on inside himself. He said it was between two wolves.

One wolf was evil: Anger, envy, sorrow, regret, greed, arrogance, self-pity, guilt, resentment, inferiority, lies, false pride, superiority, and ego.

The other wolf was good: Joy, peace, love, hope, serenity, humility, kindness, benevolence, empathy, generosity, truth, compassion, and faith.

The granddaughter thought about it for a minute and then asked her grandfather, "Which wolf will win?"

The old Cherokee simply replied, "The one I feed."

– Cherokee Story

In this chapter we will present some philosophical perspectives that determine the direction of a company's vision, values, and ethical principles. Most of the chapter is in the form of questions to help you understand your own assumptions about business ethics. If you are a manager, this understanding will help you make decisions about directing your company or group. If you are not a manager, this understanding will help you make decisions about the kind of company where you want to seek employment.

First we will look at different philosophies of the purpose of business. Next we will explore the role of government and the place of competition itself in business values. Then we will discuss corporate self-interest and the pursuit of profits.

Finally we will present the issues involved in an ownership society versus a stewardship society and raise the issue of the eroding of public trust in business.

The chapter concludes with questions for reflection.

The Purpose of Business

How often do you hear that the purpose of business is simply to make money, or specifically to make a profit for its investors?

This is the modern expression of the classic economic theory, which originated with Adam Smith and is discussed in the following section. It is so ingrained in U.S. capitalism that until recently business executives and stockholders have tended to believe either that it is right and ethical or that it is so powerful it cannot be changed. But the commitment to the classic theory is changing because of the recent scandals in business ethics, because of the "flattening" of the world by the internet and globalization, and because of the workplace spirituality movement itself. Businesses are being challenged to conduct business ethically and to consider all stakeholders world-wide, not just stockholders, in their business decisions and plans.

The Classic Theory

The economic theory held by the corporate officers usually sets the purpose of a company's business and its resulting business ethics. Classic economic capitalism and the traditional view of business are based on Adam Smith, an eighteenth century Scottish political economist and philosopher who wrote *The Wealth of Nations* in 1776.

Consumption as the Purpose of Production

It is not from the benevolence of the butcher, the brewer, or the baker, that we expect our dinner, but from their regard to their own interest. We address ourselves, not to their humanity but to their self-love, and never talk to them of our own necessities but of their advantage. . . .[1]

Every individual necessarily labors to render the annual revenue of the society as great as he can. He generally indeed neither intends to promote the public interest, nor knows how much he is promoting it. He intends only his own gain, and he is in this, as in many other cases, led by an invisible hand to promote an end which was no part of his intention. By pursuing his own interest he frequently promotes that of society more effectively than when he really intends to promote it. I have never known much good done by those who affected to trade for the public good. . . .

Consumption is the sole end and purpose of all production; and the interest of the producer ought to be attended to, only so far as it may be necessary for promoting that of the consumer. [2]

Smith's views were best expressed this way in the twenty-first and beginning of the twenty-second centuries:

The issue is the question of the purpose of corporations in society. The tradition . . . is that of capitalist minimalism: the Stanford maxim of 'the purpose of business is business.'[3]

This is the Anglo-American business model that places shareholder sovereignty above all else.[4]

Society and the "Invisible Hand"

Smith believed that the proper motive of every businessman was to use his capital for his own personal advantage, not that of society. But Smith further believed that by following his own best interests, a businessman will benefit the larger society:

Every individual is continually exerting himself to find out the most advantageous employment for whatever capital he can command. It is his own advantage, indeed, and not that of the society, which he has in view. But the study of his own advantage naturally, or rather necessarily, leads him to prefer that employment which is most advantageous to the society. . .

Every individual who employs his capital in the support of domestic industry, necessarily endeavours so to direct that industry that its [product] may be of the greatest possible value.

Smith goes on to say:

> He intends only his own gain, and he is in this, as in many other cases, **led by an invisible hand** to promote an end which was no part of his intention. Nor is it always the worse for the society that it was no part of it. By pursuing his own interest he frequently promotes that of the society more effectually than when he really intends to promote it. I have never known much good done by those who affected to trade for the public good. It is an affectation, indeed, not very common among merchants, and very few words need be employed in dissuading them from it.[5] [emphasis added]

"The butcher, the brewer, and the baker" have been replaced by multi-national corporations, whose size and wealth exceed that of many nations. Today we are well aware that many businesses create needs and desires where none would otherwise exist. Then they market their products to meet those artificially created needs and desires.

Alternative Theories

Today some theorists and business leaders are offering different perspectives on the purpose of business:

> The purpose of business is not to maximize profits for shareholders but to steward our resources to serve the world in an economically sustainable way.[6]
>
> – Dennis Bakke

R. Edward Freeman holds business accountable for moral and ethical decisions:

> We need to see business activity as a moral activity, an activity that affects the hopes and dreams and well-being of many human beings. The shareholder orthodoxy would have us believe that we can separate 'business' from 'ethics', but the real world tells us that we can't and shouldn't. Business is no different from other aspects of our lives, and we need to see executives and their stakeholders as fully fledged moral beings.

'Business ethics' should be a redundancy rather than an oxymoron.[7]

Examining Your Company's Business Model

Is the only role of business in society to pursue its own self-interest in maximizing profits?

Or is it to produce and provide goods and services that society needs? Do most businesses do this, or do they create desires in society for the things they want to produce?

Do you agree with Adam Smith's view that "consumption is the sole end and purpose of all production"?

Or do you agree with *Ethical Corporation* (EthicalCorp), which contests this view?

> The primary purpose of business is the efficient production and distribution of goods and services that society needs. The right to take profit from this social function demands justification.[8]

The way you answer these questions both reveals and affects your own and your employer's business ethics. These questions are fundamental in this time of globalization, ethics scandals, and corporate social responsibility issues.

Competition as the Highest Value for Business

Some theorists define the "rules of the game" as engaging "in open and free competition without deception or fraud." Is this the highest ethical value to which business should aspire? To quote Clive Crook,

> Today corporate social responsibility, if it is nothing else, is the tribute that capitalism everywhere pays to virtue. . . . Unopposed, the CSR movement has distilled a widespread suspicion of capitalism into a set of demands for action.[9]

Do business values matter? Stephen Jordan writes:

> Business environments that promote virtues like honesty, integrity, thriftiness, dedication, responsibility, and account-

ability lower transaction costs, build trust and teamwork, and spur productivity.[10]

Like it or not, business values do matter. As Bob Nardelli, CEO of The Home Depot®, mentioned in an interview for the Center for Corporate Citizenship newsletter,

"You can build anything and become anything with a foundation of honesty and integrity, because that will set the course." Notable thinkers like George Gilder, Francis Fukuyama, and Max Weber have all identified a connection between values and business success. Business environments that promote virtues like honesty, integrity, thriftiness, dedication, responsibility, and accountability lower transaction costs, build trust and teamwork, and spur productivity. . . .

To be sure, businesses can't take their eyes off their core competencies. . . . business success is driven by many factors, and intelligent business managers are constantly looking for the highest quality, lowest cost, most-customer-pleasing solutions they can find to do their jobs.[11]

Corporate Size and Self-interest

Can we depend on large corporations, especially multi-nationals, to run their business with the kind of self-interest that cares about their reputation for honesty or about fairness, or about paying their debts and living up to their promises?

Can we trust businesses today to look beyond short-term profit? What about your company or employer? Or the corporations whose stocks you have bought?

Can we depend on them to be, as Adam Smith believed more than two centuries ago, either rational or concerned about the public good? Have they proved themselves to have the kind of enlightened self-interest he described?

Ethical Corporation argues:

Economics is concerned with efficient resource use, not social behaviour, and [Adam] Smith knew that self-interest has to be pursued by people of conscience if public good was to be served.

In Smith's time, the dominant form of enterprise was the partnership, in which ownership and management were fused.

When the spread of public limited companies separated ownership from management, managers lost the freedom to act with conscience. Social accountability disappeared.[12]

Do the failure of communism and the success of capitalism prove that Adam Smith was right in saying that economic self-interest was best for the public interest?

Scott Garber, senior pastor of the Washington [D.C.] Community Fellowship, a multi-denominational evangelical congregation says,

According to capitalist theory, we shouldn't have to worry about the impact of self-interest, because it takes care of itself, cancels itself out. We've all heard that a rising tide lifts all boats. This is undoubtedly true of boats, but it is not necessarily true of people, because people don't float quite as naturally as boats, and boats (if left to themselves) do not try to sink their fellows.[13]

In the same sermon, Garber quotes Scott Klinger, who wrote in *The Other Side*:

Classic capitalist theory teaches that the capitalist earns her or his return for the risk she or he takes in organizing production. Yet in reality, we see most modern capitalists achieve success by putting others at risk. . . The risk of an economic downturn is no longer borne primarily by the capitalist who suffers through a recession, but by the army of workers whose jobs are sacrificed in order to preserve profits.[14]

Upholding the classic view of capitalism, *The Economist* is careful to distinguish between greed and self-interest:

Greed and self-interest are not the same thing. . . . Greed, in the ordinary meaning of the word, is not rational or calculating. Freely indulged, it makes you fat and drives you into bankruptcy. The kind of self-interest that advances the public good is rational and enlightened.[15]

Patricia Aburdene explains the difference between greed and enlightened self-interest:

Greed is self-interest run amok. When greed takes over, we are out of Balance. We sacrifice the other and the whole to our selfishness. And as a result, our own self-interest, rather than thriving, suffers.[16]

The Pursuit of Profits—Good, Evil, or Neutral?

What do you think of Milton Friedman's argument? He opposes

the already too prevalent view that the pursuit of profits is wicked and immoral and must be curbed and controlled by external forces. Once this view is adopted, the external forces that curb the market will not be the social consciences, however highly developed, of the pontificating executives; it will be the iron fist of Government bureaucrats.[17]

Is this the only alternative?

Tim McGuire challenges the value of short-term profits as an indicator of business growth and success and also challenges the assumption that stockholders are really the owners of a company:

It is very hard to properly classify companies by their behavior, but there a lot of indications that short-term profits do not guarantee long-term success. . . .

The equation that stock price equals success implies that rewarding stockholders is the same as rewarding owners. That may give us a distorted view of corporations. Marjorie Kelley, the author of . . . *The Divine Right to Capital,* argues that only one in every 100 stockholder dollars goes to the company. The rest, she says is speculative dollars "gambled among fellow shareholders." Stockholders are not owners the way the shoemaker and the candlemakers owned their businesses. They are more gambler than owner. . . . .

Measurement of profit is easy. Measuring how much a company damages the environment, a community's self image or a local economy is far more difficult to assess. . . .

Obsession with quarterly profits may put a lot of money in a few executives' pockets and it may make a company look exciting for a short time, it is definitely not the only way to measure a company's success.[18]

On the other hand, as Aburdene points out, "oldline, profit-at-any-cost capitalism" is supported by the law in the United States:

> Public companies, as lawful entities under state code, are required to conduct business so as to *maximize* shareholder profits. . . . Public companies, it would appear, are legally obliged to engage in a destructive form of capitalism.[19]

Aburdene maintains that the emerging megatrend of Conscious Capitalism

> holds that business bears moral and ethical responsibilities beyond short-term profit and maximum shareholder return. Equally important, it lifts the frequency of free enterprise from self-interest to the higher octave of enlightened self-interest . . . . It asks: If I act in my own self-interest and keep doing so, what are the ramifications of my choices? Which acts—that may look fine right now—will come around and injure me and others one year from now? Ten years? Twenty-five years?[20]

Ownership vs. Stewardship

Classic economic capitalism seeks to protect the philosophical value of ownership and an ownership society. This position argues that corporations and their managers ought not to be held accountable to stakeholders because such accountability would undermine the concept of ownership by giving equal status to non-owners.

An ownership society is defined by the Cato Institute as a society that

> values responsibility, liberty, and property. Individuals are empowered by freeing them from dependence on government handouts and making them owners instead, in control of their own lives and destinies. In the ownership society, patients control their own health care, parents control their own children's education, and workers control their retirement savings.[21]

What is ownership? Should individuals own everything? Should communities be the owners, as has been the case with indigenous and tribal peoples? Should governments be the owners? What should the limits be? Who makes the rules? What do *you* have to gain or to lose?

In the blog entry, "The Kingdom of God is not an 'Ownership Society' " a blogger identified only as *jj* asks

> What is ownership? Having been a student of Property Law, I can tell you that there is consensus among judges and commentators that the nature of ownership boils down to one thing: the right to exclude others. . . . In other words, my watch is my watch because I can keep you from using or taking it. My house is my house because I can keep you from entering it. Remember that my argument about the nature of ownership is not about how things should be. I'm merely describing things as they are. When judges enforce "property rights" or "ownership," this is what they enforce: "keep out" or "keep off" rights. I can eat my sandwich even if I don't need it and you do. . . .
>
> A powerful objection to my analysis is that it is tantamount to advocating pure socialism. But socialism does not necessarily follow from the analysis. The question is one of starting point: what is our beginning value, our first principle, from which all other rules will be seen as exceptions. There will certainly be taxation and welfare—social sharing—in [President] Bush's "ownership society." But this sharing is conceptualized as an exception to the norm of ownership and exclusion; as necessary to serve what Bush sees as values subordinate to private property rights, such as economic equality.[22]

What alternatives might we have to seeing ourselves and our highest values as those of ownership?

Bill May, an advocate of a stewardship model makes this plea:

> We urge the country to dig deeper into its ideals than the current slogan of an ownership society and recover its responsibilities as a stewardship society. At present, we are an ownership society on the credit card, building up huge deficits and trade deficits that undercut our covenant with the future. At the same time, a stewardship society must acknowledge that each fundamental good, such as health care, competes

with other fundamental goods such as education and public safety. Thus the wise and efficient use of public funds is not simply an economic but a moral necessity.[23]

Stockholders vs. Stakeholders

For a number of years, many corporations have put profit-making as their primary, or only, purpose. Stockholders were the only stakeholders they tried to please. Today more companies realize that they must consider *all* their stakeholders if they want more than temporary success.

In addition to stockholders, stakeholders include employees, contractors and vendors, customers, the local community, the nation, and the world

Some companies act as though the inclusion of all stakeholders is necessary as a part of public relations, but more and more companies seek to be genuinely ethical and socially responsible. Chapter 10 discusses the "stockholder vs. stakeholder" debate and other issues related to corporate social responsibility.

The "business of business is business" philosophy ignores the fact that social issues are fundamental to business and can point to factors that do, or soon will, affect its profitability.

Restoring Public Trust

Trust is a critical factor in the conduct of your business with all your constituents. A lack of trust on the part of your employees can sabotage your productivity, a lack of trust on the part of your consumers can ruin your sales, and a lack of trust on the part of your investors can cost you capital.

The 2005 Edelman Trust Barometer indicated that leaders are withdrawing their trust of CEOs, heads of state, and other institutional leaders.[24] As credibility, respect, and fairness have faltered among institutional leaders, opinion leaders are turning to a personal web of trust that includes "colleagues," "friends and family," "a person like yourself" as well as independent experts such as doctors and academics.

About 90% of them reject advertising as a source of trustworthy information, and give only qualified acceptance to information found in articles and news stories:

More than 80% of respondents overall do not believe information unless they see or hear it from multiple sources.[25]

Questions for Reflection

1. What do you think is the role of business in society?

2. Which secular institution in our society should be in the forefront of social justice—business or government? Or some other group?

3. Discuss profit and competition in our society.

4. Do the failure of communism and the success of capitalism prove that Adam Smith was right in saying that economic self-interest was best for the public interest?

5. What is ownership? Should individuals own everything? Should communities be the owners, as has been the case with indigenous and tribal peoples? Should governments be the owners? What should be the limits? Who makes the rules? What do *you* have to gain or to lose?

6. Discuss why trust in business has eroded so much and how trust might be restored.

Looking Ahead

Chapter 9, "Corporate Social Responsibility continues the discussion of ethics by defining Corporate Social Responsibility (CSR), exploring various meanings of CSR and discussing your business' constituent groups.

Endnotes

1 Adam Smith, *An Inquiry into the Nature and Causes of the Wealth of Nations*. London: Methuen and Co., Ltd., ed. Edwin Cannan, 1904. [Online] available from http://www.econlib.org/library/Smith/smWN1.html (Accessed November 28, 2005)
2 Smith, *op cit.*, http://www.econlib.org/library/Smith/smWN13.html
3 Maxim attributed to Milton Friedman.
4 Dr. Peter Wells, "Bhopal: the disaster continues," Cardiff Business School, Cardiff Centre for Ethics Law and Society, Issue of the Month for January 2005, http://www.ccels.cf.ac.uk/literature/issue/2005/pwells.pdf, (Accessed August 19, 2005)
5 Smith, *op cit.*
6 http://www.bluestratus.net/sites/JoyAtWork/bakketop10 (Accessed July 15, 2005)
7 R. Edward Freeman, "Foreword" in *Unfolding Stakeholder Thinking, Vol. I: Theory, Responsibility and Engagement*, http://www.greenleaf-publishing.com/catalogue/unfold.htm#chdownload (Accessed January 11, 2005)
8 "Leaders: Bad arguments against the good company? – A response to *The Economist* regarding the relationship between business and society." *Ethical Corporation* magazine editorial, January 31 2005
9 Clive Crook, "The good company," from: SURVEY: CORPORATE SOCIAL RESPONSIBILITY, *The Economist* print edition http://www.economist.com/displaystory.cfm?story_id=3555212 (Accessed Jan 20th 2005)
10 Stephen Jordan, Editorial – "Taking Issue With the Economist's CSR Issue," Center for Corporate Citizenship, http://www.uschamber.com/bclc/media/2005/jan-feb/default#editorial (Accessed June 16, 2005 and January 27, 2006)
11 *Ibid.*
12 http://www.ethicalcorp.com/content.asp?ContentID=3420
13 Scott Garber, "How to Be a Christian in a Capitalist World," http://www.scottgarber.com/ChristianCapitalist.pdf (Accessed February 24, 2005)
14 Scott Klinger, "The Corporate Body and the Body of Christ," *The Other Side* magazine (Volume 40, Number 1)
15 "Profit and the public good," *The Economist* print edition, Jan 20th, 2005, http://www.economist.com/PrinterFriendly.cfm?Story_ID=3555259 (Accessed June 2005)

16 Patricia Aburdene, *Megatrends 2010: The Rise of Conscious Capitalism* (Charlottesville, VA: Hampton Roads Publishing Company, 2005), p. 163
17 Milton, Friedman, "The Social Responsibility of Business is to Increase its Profits" *The New York Times Magazine*, September 13, 1970. http://www.colorado.edu/studentgroups/libertarians/issues/friedman-soc-resp-business.html (Accessed August 20, 2005)
18 Tim McGuire, "More than Work" column for May 30, 2005, http://www.timjmcguire.com/columns_output.asp?columnID=39 (Accessed July 14, 2005) Copyright 2005, More than Work Distributed by United Feature Syndicate, Inc.
19 Aburdene, *op. cit.,* p. 173-174
20 *Ibid.,* p. 175
21 http://www.cato.org/special/ownership_society/ (Accessed July 14, 2005)
22 jj, "The Kingdom of God is not an 'Ownership Society,'" *Social Gospel Today,* http://socialgospel.blogspot.com/2004/12/kingdom-of-god-is-not-ownership.html (Accessed July 19, 2005)
23 Bill May, edited transcript of a talk to Charlottesville & Albemarle Democrats, April 16, 2005, http://loper.org/~george/archives/2005/May/894.html (Accessed July 19, 2005)
24 The annual Edelman Trust Barometer is a survey of 1500 opinion leaders in key markets in the United States, Europe, and Japan. Edelman is the world's largest independent public relations firm.
25 "Trust Shifting From Traditional Authorities to Peers, Edelman Trust Barometer Finds" http://www.prnewswire.com/cgi-bin/stories.pl?ACCT=109&STORY=/www/story/01-24-2005/0002898452&EDATE (Accessed February 10, 2005)

9 Corporate Social Responsibility

COWS NEVER DIE

The practice of ukasisa or "cows never die" comes from Zimbabwe. When a poor person in the community is encountered, the dignity of that person is protected by someone better endowed with cattle-wealth communicating the need for one of his or her cows to be cared for. This transaction in turn provides the destitute member with milk and wealth in the form of one or two calves, after which the original cow is "borrowed back."[1]

~~~~~~

To survive in the twenty-first century, companies have to move beyond their aggressive, competitive tendencies and learn to be not only sociable, but genuinely concerned about the perspectives and wellbeing of *all* of their stakeholders; not just shareholders, but also employees, communities, customers, suppliers and civil society organisations.[2]

- Wayne Visser

~~~~~~

Chapter 7 addressed the basic ethical elements of business as expressed through a company's vision, values, and ethical principles. The major focus of Chapter 7 was on the purpose, honesty, and ethics of a company's financial dealings, reporting, and accountability.

Chapter 8 provided a philosophical basis for business ethics in preparation for expanding the discussion. This chapter continues the discussion of ethics by defining Corporate Social Responsibility

(CSR). We will explore various meanings of CSR and discuss your business' constituent groups.

Finally, we will present examples of some specific companies that have received awards for excellence in one or more areas of corporate social responsibility above and beyond the financial bottom line.

What Is Corporate Social Responsibility?

> Not everything that can be counted counts, and not everything that counts can be counted.
>
> — Albert Einstein

Corporate Social Responsibility (CSR) extends beyond volunteerism, charity, philanthropy, and cause-related marketing. CSR is defined in several ways:

- As a holistic approach to corporate ethics

- As a "triple bottom line"

- As determined by all of a corporation's constituencies, or stakeholders

A Holistic Approach to Corporate Ethics

A holistic approach to CSR incorporates sustainable development, which is defined as "development which meets the needs of the present without compromising the ability of future generations to meet their own needs."[3]

In 1992 approximately 50 companies joined to form Business for Social Responsibility (BSR) to marry commercial success and social responsibility. Among the founders of BSR were Ben & Jerry's™, Patagonia® and Tom's™ of Maine.

BSR's mission was and is

> to create a just and sustainable global economy by working with companies to promote more responsible business practices, innovation and collaboration.[4]

Witnessing and experiencing the expansion of global trade, more businesses and their stakeholders have discovered how globalization affects local communities as well as nations, the environment of countries and of the whole world, and issues of human rights. As these issues have grown in importance to regulators and consumers, they have become more relevant to investors and financial markets, too. Today Business for Social Responsibility (BSR) provides a large collection of tools and resources, including briefs on a variety of ethical issues, to help its members and the public at large.[5] It describes itself as

> a global organization that helps member companies achieve success in ways that respect ethical values, people, communities and the environment. . . .A nonprofit organization, BSR promotes cross sector collaboration and contributes to global efforts to advance the field of corporate social responsibility.[6]

BSR understands Corporate Social Responsibility (CSR) as a holistic approach to business that accepts the responsibilities of full partnership with its community. It defines CSR as

> achieving commercial success in ways that honor ethical values and respect people, communities, and the natural environment. . . . CSR means addressing the legal, ethical, commercial and other expectations society has for business, and making decisions that fairly balance the claims of all key stakeholders. . . . and includes responsibility for current and past actions as well as future impacts. . . . In its broadest categories, CSR typically includes issues related to: business ethics, community investment, environment, governance, human rights, marketplace and workplace.[7]

The World Business Council for Sustainable Development (WBCSD) is an organization of 180 international companies who have "a shared commitment to sustainable development via the three pillars of economic growth, ecological balance and social progress."[8] The council relates CSR to sustainable development as follows:

> As an engine for social progress, Corporate Social Responsibility (CSR) helps companies live up to their responsibilities as global citizens and local neighbors in a fast-changing world.
>
> We define CSR as "business' commitment to contribute to sustainable economic development, working with employees, their families, the local community, and society at large to improve their quality of life." We are convinced that a coherent CSR strategy, based on integrity, sound values, and a long-term approach offers clear business benefits to companies and contributes to the well-being of society.[9]

CSR and the Triple Bottom Line

Many companies are beginning to speak of corporate social responsibility in terms of the "triple bottom line." Coined by John Elkington in his book *Cannibals with Forks: The Triple Bottom Line of 21st Century Business*, this phrase refers to a framework for measuring and reporting corporate performance against economic, social, and environmental parameters.[10] Elkington founded SustainAbility™, "a strategy consultancy and independent think-tank specialising in the business risks and market opportunities of corporate responsibility and sustainable development."

> Sustainable development is about safeguarding the world for future generations. We work with business to deliver sustainability by helping them manage and measure their success not just on the basis of profit, but across what we've termed the 'triple bottom line' of economic, social and environmental performance. . . . For a business to be profitable and deliver long-term shareholder value it must manage across—and increasingly blend—all three of these dimensions. To do this, a business must engage with key stakeholders and innovate sustainable solutions—not just manage risks. Transparency and integrity are central, comprising key elements of corporate responsibility. [11]

Corporate social responsibility requires a long-term commitment to do business in ways that preserve or enhance, rather than harm, the surrounding community, employees, the environment and economic systems.[12]

CSR and Multiple Constituencies

In the past 20 years, businesses have come to recognize that they have other stakeholders besides their stockholders. They have learned that they must consider more than a single constituency. Though the number of constituencies varies according to the count, acknowledging multiple constituencies has changed the way that corporations must do business.

Four Constituencies

In the 1980's, much was made of the fact that an executive's sole constituency in a public corporation is the shareholders,[13] and therefore that maximizing shareholder value was the exclusive goal. This message was always heard in the context of the leveraged buy-out and break-up of a corporation as a rationale for its destruction. It was not a long-term philosophy.

A corporation, public or private, which desires to stay in business long-term, as opposed to one which is closing up tomorrow, has four constituencies: **its employees, its clients, its shareholders and the public in general.** The philosophy of "maximizing shareholder value" suggests that you can do so by exploiting or even by destroying the other three groups. The opposite is true. In most cases, shareholder value is maximized in the long term only when the other three constituencies are being cared for properly. The healthy organization is one which regards all four constituencies as ends, not means.[14] [emphasis added]

Seven Constituencies

For five years, *Business Ethics* magazine has recognized the 100 Best Corporate Citizens in terms of their service to a variety of stakeholders. Here the number of stakeholders rises to seven:

Service to a variety of stakeholders is the essence of good corporate citizenship. That's what the 100 Best Corporate Citizens listing is about. While traditional measures of success focus on stockholder return, this list defines success more broadly. Using social ratings compiled by KLD Research & Analytics of Boston—plus total return to shareholders—our list ranks companies according to service to seven stakeholder groups: **stockholders, community, minorities and women, employees, environment, non-U.S. stakeholders, and customers.** Good corporate citizens serve all constituencies well. That's the emerging definition of corporate success.[15] [emphasis added]

Considering each of these seven stakeholders groups is one measure your business can use to evaluate its growth in the area of corporate social responsibility.

Your Traditional Constituents: Stockholders

The most traditional stakeholder group, which used to be considered the *only* stakeholder group, is your stockholders (also called shareholders). Now however, research in both Canada and the United States shows that "over the long term, companies that rate highest on ethics and corporate social responsibility are the most profitable."[16]

A Morgan Stanley/Oekom study of the financial performance of 600 global Morgan Stanley Capital International (MCSI) companies between 1999 and 2003 found that an index of "best in class" companies, based on rigorous environmental and social performance measures, outperformed an index of "sustainability laggards" by 23%.[17]

A study by Dr. Marc Orlitzky of the Australian Graduate School of Management (AGSM) shows that companies that incorporate and internalize socially responsible behavior are likely to have a stronger financial bottom line than companies that ignore their social responsibility or merely pay lip service to it. Commenting on the research,

Orlitzky states that most companies must change their thinking from viewing social responsibility as a cost to business:

> To reap the full economic rewards of CSR, companies will have to integrate their activities into their strategic decision-making processes and ethical cultures. The data reveals that the highest performers were those corporations that did not think of stakeholders as forces to be 'managed' by public relations, but that took their moral obligations to all the communities in which they operate very seriously.
>
> My research adds to the growing evidence that when corporations are good citizens, business risk decreases—for both large and small firms.[18]

In other words, it is as important for a corporation to walk the walk as it is for an individual to do so.

Your Closest Constituents: Employees

Each year the Great Place To Work® Institute produces various "Best Companies" lists, both in the U.S. and in other countries. The Great Place to Work Institute defines a great place to work as one in which you "trust the people you work for, have pride in what you do, and enjoy the people you work with."[19]

The relationship between management and employees must be one of trust. Their website defines the dimensions of a Great Place to Work as follows:

> **Trust** is the essential ingredient for the primary workplace relationship between the employee and the employer. According to our model, trust is composed of three dimensions: Credibility, Respect, and Fairness.
>
> **Credibility** means managers regularly communicate with employees about the company's direction and plans—and solicit their ideas. It involves coordinating people and resources efficiently and effectively, so that employees know how their work relates to the company's goals. It's the integrity management brings to the business. To be credible, words must be followed by action.

Respect involves providing employees with the equipment, resources, and training they need to do their job. It means appreciating good work and extra effort. It includes reaching out to employees and making them partners in the company's activities, fostering a spirit of collaboration across departments and creating a work environment that's safe and healthy. Respect means that work/life balance is a practice, not a slogan.

At an organisation that's **fair**, economic success is shared equitably through compensation and benefit programs. Everybody receives equitable opportunity for recognition. Decisions on hiring and promotions are made impartially, and the workplace seeks to free itself of discrimination, with clear processes for appealing and adjudicating disputes. To be fair, you must be just.

The final two dimensions of the Institute's model relate to workplace relationships between employees and their jobs/company (**Pride**), and between the employee and other employees (**Camaraderie**).

As companies become great, the division between management and labour fades. The workplace becomes a community. Employees take pride in their job, their team, and their company. They feel that they can be themselves at work. They celebrate the successes of their peers and cooperate with others throughout the organisation. People take pleasure in their work—and in the people they work with—in a deep and lasting way. They want to stay around for their careers.[20]

In "The case against job satisfaction—a satisfied worker is not necessarily a productive worker,"[21] Glenn Bassett claims that statistical studies fail to support the assumption that satisfied workers are productive workers. He further concludes that the connection between employee satisfaction and productivity may never be proved by research alone. Bassett believes that depending on worker satisfaction to preserve or improve productivity is naïve and risky for business and that the purpose of human relations in business should not be seen as a way to increase productivity but as a way to be in harmony with society's evolving values and labor's increased expectations.

Amy Lyman[22] of The Great Place to Work® Institute explains that

> satisfaction is a baseline finding that is not related to productivity, yet the level of trust as we measure it has shown interesting correlations with firm performance. The most direct evidence that we share on our website comes from studies conducted by the Russell Investment Group (http://www.greatplacetowork.com/great/graphs.php). So we see benefits to high trust companies that come in both the realm of being in harmony with society's changing values and in the realm of financial performance.[23]

Other Constituents With Personal Contact

> The secret of success is honesty and fair dealing. If you can fake these, you've got it made.
>
> – Mark Twain

Corporate social responsibility within the immediate context of your company includes responsibility to your company's closest constituents — those who come in and out of your company building or are in contact with your business by phone. Besides your employees, these constituents include contractors, vendors and suppliers, and clients and customers. All of these constituents deserve the same thorough integrity, credibility, respect, and fairness that you should give your employees.

What about your supply chain?

Your company's responsibility also extends to research and development. Are the products and services you offer to clients and customers useful, helpful, and not harmful?

Corporate social responsibility toward your nearest constituents extends to the marketplace. It includes the honesty and integrity with which you describe and market your products and services. It also includes the fairness of your pricing structure and the fairness and honesty of any comments you and your company make about your competitors.

Constituents Beyond Personal Contact

Most businesses now realize that their ethical responsibility—their corporate social responsibility—extends to constituents beyond their immediate business. These constituents, or stakeholders, include your neighbors and community, your environment and the global community.

Two of the principles David Batstone raises in his book *Saving the Corporate Soul* address your company's relationships with the human constituents beyond your building.

> A company will think of itself as part of a community as well as a market.[24]

> A company will pursue international trade and production based on respect for the rights of workers and citizens of trade partner nations.[25]

But your company also has responsibility toward the environment, which includes both the products and byproducts of your business. As Batstone puts it:

> The environment will be treated as a silent stakeholder, a party to which the company is wholly accountable.[26]

Your corporate responsibility also includes the environment in which your products are used. For example, your production plant may not discharge any damaging waste into water, earth, or air, but do your products themselves damage the environment through emissions or electronic components containing dangerous metals?

Your Global Constituents

What is the impact of your company on other nations, their people, and their physical environment? Most companies have some trade with other countries, whether as suppliers or workers or customers. Corporate social responsibility recognizes that a company, as well as an individual person, is part of the larger context.

Albert Einstein described this relationship well:

A human being is part of a whole, called by us the Universe. . . He experiences himself, his thoughts and feelings, as something separated from the rest—a kind of optical delusion of his consciousness. This delusion is a kind of prison for us. . . . Our task must be to free ourselves from this prison by widening our circles of compassion to embrace all living creatures and the whole of nature in its beauty.

– Albert Einstein

Pierre Teilhard de Chardin,[27] a Jesuit paleontologist, philosopher and mystic, was another visionary thinker whose writings provide a philosophical basis for the internet, globalization, and new evolutionary theories:

No one can deny that a network (a world network) of economic and psychic affiliations is being woven at ever increasing speed which envelops and constantly penetrates more deeply within each of us. With every day that passes it becomes a little more impossible for us to act or think otherwise than collectively. [28]

No One Gets It All Right

In describing the 2004 *Business Ethics* list of 100 Best Corporate Citizens, Peter Asmus readily admits that there are criticisms and controversies in the selection. For example, Eastman Kodak™ Company received high marks for its anti-discrimination policies in hiring and tied for the top in service to its employees, but its environmental policies fell short.

In December 2003, Eastman Kodak (No. 58) was targeted by the Citizen's Environmental Coalition for air emissions and on-site hazardous waste incinerators[29]

Other controversies:

In 2003, a federal judge ruled that IBM (No. 12) had discriminated against older employees in converting to a cash-balance pension program. Washington Mutual (No. 29) has been accused of predatory lending. . . . Both Timberland (No. 17) and Sara Lee (No. 87) have faced accusations of unhealthy working conditions at overseas factories. [30]

Recognition of a business for its achievements in one aspect of CSR does not mean it is necessarily outstanding in all areas. As Asmus says:

> This list is not a certification of flawlessness. . . . In the end, the 100 Best Corporate Citizens list aims to make a simple point: excellence in business is about more than profits for shareholders —it's about serving a variety of stakeholders well. To put it another way, it's about having your good deeds outweigh your misdeeds. Judged against their peers among the nation's largest public companies, these 100 companies have risen to the top.[31]

Perhaps pointing out those areas of success can provide goals and role models for your own corporation. At least they should provide stimulus for thinking and for ethical discussion within your company.

Companies Recognized for CSR

The following companies have received recognition for one or more aspects of their corporate social responsibility. The award criteria used by the groups that honored these companies are listed in Appendix A.

Chiquita™ Brands International, Inc.

Chiquita™ Brands International, Inc., based in the United States, is the world's top banana producer. It is a recognized leader in its "institutionalized CSR management structure, rigorous labor and environmental standards, committed participation in international certification programs, industry-leading labor agreements, and candid sustainability reports."[32] According to Chiquita's web page on Corporate Responsibility,

> Chiquita has reaffirmed its commitment to respect the core labor conventions of the ILO by signing the historic agreement on "Freedom of Association, Minimum Labour Standards and

Employment in Latin American Banana Operations." The full text of this agreement is available in English and Spanish.

Chiquita's commitment to the environment is also reflected in our having achieved 100% certification of our owned farms to the environmental and social standards of the Rainforest Alliance, the international standard for environmental protection and for worker health and safety in our banana farms. . . .

Chiquita is also a member of the UK-based Ethical Trading Initiative. The ETI is a unique alliance of companies, non-governmental organizations and labor unions working together to advance good practice in business ethics, corporate responsibility and human rights. [33]

In 2004 Chiquita won the Corporate Citizen of the Americas Award for its home-ownership project in Honduras. The Organization of American States (OAS), through its not-for-profit arm Trust for the Americas, established the award to reward and encourage corporate efforts to alleviate poverty in the Americas.

Starbucks Coffee Co.

BSR lists Starbucks as another example of CSR leadership, describing its approach to corporate social responsibility as follows:

Starbucks defines CSR as conducting business in ways that produce social, environmental and economic benefits to the communities where they operate. Starbucks has been widely recognized for its commitment to numerous stakeholders including coffee growers, the environment, employees, and communities, while simultaneously achieving rapid financial growth. . . . Since 1998, Starbucks has supported Conservation International's (CI) Conservation Coffee program, which encourages sustainable agriculture practices and the protection of biodiversity through the production of shade-grown coffee and the institution of coffee purchasing guidelines. . . . The company has also been praised for its generous employee benefits and its commitment, unusual in the industry, to provide full benefits to both full and part-time employees. Starbucks has taken a leadership role by being the first coffee company to adopt a "framework for a code of conduct" to improve the quality of life for workers globally. [34]

Novo Nordisk A/S®

In contrast with the current (2004-2006) ethical issues being discovered in many large drug companies, Novo Nordisk is an example, at the time of this writing, of a highly respected and successful pharmaceutical company. Based in Denmark and specializing in diabetes care, Novo is viewed as a leader in CSR in its efforts to achieve a triple bottom line for the past 10 years.

> Novo uses an aggressive stakeholder engagement program that seeks to learn the needs and concerns of Novo's stakeholders, such as diabetics, employees and the environment, to direct its CSR activities. Novo also invests in partnerships that seek to address these social and environmental goals [and is committed] to a standard of sustainable business practices covering workplace standards, environmental management and human rights. . . . For more than a decade, Novo has followed a proactive environmental policy aiming to be one of the front-runners in defining, engaging and reporting on how business can address global environmental challenges. In its latest undertaking, Novo is implementing the ISO 14001 environmental management structure at all of its production facilities with staff working continuously to reduce the consumption of resources such as clean water and fossil fuels.[35]

Novo was strongly criticized for joining an industry-wide action against the government to protect its patents in South Africa. After reflecting on the criticism, the company addressed the challenge "to help lessen the global inequities in health care." In response,

> [Novo] established the LEAD initiative (Leadership in Education and Access to Diabetes care), which aims to improve diabetes care in developing countries. One LEAD initiative is the World Partner Program, which has evaluated the dilemma diabetes causes in developing nations. Another element of LEAD is the establishment of the World Diabetes Foundation, through which the company will donate approximately $73 million over the next ten years.[36]

The Novo website states:

> Novo Nordisk is actively seeking to promote social respon-
> sibility and a good environmental performance across our
> business operations. We believe that people should be treated
> fairly and that the impact on the environment should be
> minimised. We do this not only to manage our risk effectively
> but also because we think it is the right thing to do. As a truly
> responsible business, we should be able to account for all our
> activities. If our suppliers are found to be environmentally and
> socially negligent, it reflects badly on us. We therefore expect
> our suppliers to comply with both local legislation and
> international standards on environmental management and
> human rights. [37]

Regarding sustainability, Novo Nordisk says:

> Sustainable Development is about preserving the planet while
> improving the quality of life for its current and future
> inhabitants. . . . In all our work we strive to be economically
> viable, socially responsible and environ-mentally sound.
> Balancing the Triple Bottom Line is about considering each of
> these elements when making business decisions. Thereby, we
> do not only manage a sound business—we also demonstrate
> our commitment to being a driver towards sustainable
> development—globally and locally.[38]

Novo Nordisk's triple bottom line aims to be:

- Financially and economically viable regarding corporate growth, investors, and national growth
- Environmentally sound regarding the environment, animal welfare, and bioethics
- Socially responsible towards employees, people whose healthcare needs we serve, and local communities and the global community[39]

Looking Ahead

Chapter 10, "The Global Perspective: Issues in CSR" concludes Part III by considering the global implications and current debates about Corporate Social Responsibility.

Endnotes

1 Wayne Visser quoting Zimbabwean businessman and author Lovemore Mbigi about the the practice of *ukisisa*. See Wayne Visser, "Afrocentric business in Southern Aftrica," *Perspectives on Business and Global Change,* Journal of the World Business Academy, Vol. 11 No. 3, September 1997, http://www.waynevisser.com/afrocentric.htm

2 Wayne Visser, "In Search of Business on the Elephant Trail," Originally published by *Namaste,* Volume 21, July/August 2003, http://www.waynevisser.com/elephant_trail_print.htm (Accessed January 25, 2005

3 www.sustainableag.net/glossary_r-z.htm (Accessed February 18, 2005)

4 "Mission," Business for Social Responsibility, http://www.bsr.org/Meta/about/Mission.cfm (Accessed February 18, 2005)

5 "Issue Briefs," Business for Social Responsibility, http://www.bsr.org/CSRResources/index.cfm (Accessed February 18, 2005)

6 "About BSR," Business for Social Responsibility, http://www.bsr.org/Meta/About/index.cfm (Accessed February 8, 2005)

7 "Overview of Corporate Social Responsibility," Business for Social Responsibility, http://www.bsr.org/CSRResources/IssueBriefDetail.cfm?DocumentID=48809 (Accessed February 8, 2005)

8 http://www.wbcsd.ch/templates/TemplateWBCSD5/layout.asp?type=p&MenuId=NjA&doOpen=1&ClickMenu=LeftMenu (Accessed February 20, 2006) See also "WBCSD Annual Review 2004 - A decade of action and learning" at http://www.wbcsd.org/plugins/DocSearch/details.asp?type=DocDet&Objectid=MTM1NTM (Accessed February 28, 2006)

9 "Corporate Social Responsibility," World Business Council for Sustainable Development, http://www.wbcsd.ch/templates/TemplateWBCSD1/layout.asp?type=p&MenuId=MzI3&doOpen=1&ClickMenu=LeftMenu (Accessed January 3, 2005)

10 New Society Publishers, 1998

11 SustainAbility™ Online, http://www.sustainability.com/news-media/news-resource.asp?id=209 (Accessed January 13, 2006)

12 "What Is Corporate Social Responsibility?" Ethics in Action, http://www.ethicsinaction.com/whatiscsr/qanda.html (Accessed February 11, 2005)

13 *Shareholder* and *stockholder* are used interchangeably.

14 Jonathan Wallace, "Leadership," The Ethical Spectacle, October, 1998, http://www.spectacle.org/1098/leader.html (Accessed February 12, 2005)

15 Peter Asmus, "2004 100 Best Corporate Citizens," Business Ethics, http://www.business-ethics.com/100best.htm#Article (Accessed February 12, 2005)

16 "What Is Corporate Social Responsibility?" Ethics in Action, http://www.ethicsinaction.com/whatiscsr/qanda.html (Accessed February 11, 2005)

17 "Corporate Social Responsibility," Edelman, http://www.edelman.com/ expertise/practices/csr/ (Accessed February 9, 2005)

18 Marc Orlitzky, "Corporate Social Responsibility," Australian Research Council, Centre for Corporate Change, (AGSM), http://www2.agsm.edu.au/ agsm/web.nsf/AttachmentsByTitle/A02_Overview_MOrlitzky_CSR.pdf/ $FILE/A02_Overview_MOrlitzky_CSR.pdf, p. 4-5 (Accessed January 16, 2005)

19 "Our Model," Great Place to Work®, http://www.greatplacetowork.com/ great/model.php (Accessed February 18, 2005)

20 "The Dimensions of a Great Place to Work®" Great Place to Work®, http://www.greatplacetowork.com/great/dimensions.php (Accessed February 18, 2005)

21 In *Business Horizons*, May-June, 1994

22 Co-founder and currently Chair of the Board of Directors and Chair of the Strategy Committee for the Great Place to Work® Institute

23 Email to the author.

24 David Batstone, *Saving the Corporate Soul... Eight Principles for Creating and Preserving Integrity and Profitability Without Selling Out* (San Francisco:Jossey-Bass, an Imprint of Wiley, 2003), p. 73

25 *Ibid.* p. 208

26 *Ibid.* p. 154

27 1881-1955

28 Pierre Teilhard de Chardin, "The Formation of the Noosphere," *The Future of Man* (NY:Harper and Row, 1969)

29 "2004 100 Best Corporate Citizens" by Peter Asmus, http://www.business-ethics.com/100best.htm#Article (Accessed February 12, 2005)

30 *Ibid.*

31 *Ibid.*

32 http://www.bsr.org/CSRResources/IssueBriefDetail.cfm?DocumentID= 48809 (Accessed February 8, 2005)

33 See http://www.chiquita.com/ and click Corporate Responsibility. (Accessed February 8, 2005)

34 BSR's "Overview of Corporate Social Responsibility" http://www.bsr.org/ CSRResources/IssueBriefDetail.cfm?DocumentID=48809 (Accessed February 8, 2005)

35 *Ibid.*

36 *Ibid.*

37 "Commitments", Novo Nordisk, http://suppliertoolbox.novonordisk.com/ background/background.asp (Accessed February 11, 2005)

38 "Sustainability in Short," Novo Nordisk, http://www.novonordisk.com/ sustainability/sustainability_in_short/default.asp (Accessed February 11, 2005)

39 "The Triple Bottom Line" graphic, Novo Nordisk,
http://www.novonordisk.com/images/Sustainability/sr02/table_p04.gif
(Accessed February 11, 2005)

10 The Global Perspective: Issues in CSR

KING MIDAS

Once upon a time there was a king named Midas, who was extremely rich. In fact, King Midas had more riches than anyone else in the whole world, but he wanted even more! He especially wanted GOLD! He set aside a special room just to hold his gold.

In fact, the king loved his gold so much, that eventually he loved gold more than anything else in the world. He loved gold even more than he loved his daughter Marigold! His goal in life was to get more and more gold.

One day a wizard came to him and said, "I have come to grant you one wish. What is your request?"

"Gold is the best thing in the whole world!" replied the king. "I wish that everything I touch would become gold!"

"But you are already the wealthiest man in the world. You have more gold than anyone else!" protested the wizard.

"But I want more!" said the king

"Very well," said the wizard. "Beginning tomorrow, everything you touch will become gold."

The next morning, the king's wish began to be fulfilled. His bed turned to gold. So did his table and chair. The king was overjoyed! He ran through the palace, touching everything and turning it into gold.

But when King Midas sat down to eat his breakfast, his food and water also turned to cold, hard gold. There was nothing that he could swallow!

Just then his daughter Marigold came into the room. But when the king kissed her, she turned into a golden statue! The king became terrified as he realized what he had done. He called the wizard who had granted his wish.

"Please take away the gift you gave me!" he begged. "Take anything of mine that you want, but give my daughter Marigold back to me!"

"Is gold still the most important thing in the world to you?" the wizard inquired.

"No! No! I hate the sight of it" screamed the king.

So the wizard gave the king a pitcher to fill with water to use to sprinkle everything he had turned to gold. The king followed the wizard's instructions eagerly and was once again able to embrace his loving daughter and taste fresh bread and clear, pure water!

ⰻⰻⰻⰻⰻⰻⰻⰻⰻⰻⰻⰻⰻⰻⰻⰻⰻⰻⰻⰻⰻⰻⰻⰻⰻⰻⰻⰻⰻⰻⰻⰻⰻⰻ

As difficult as ethical issues can be when they relate to traditional business functions, issues of corporate social responsibility are even more complex. Too often the focus on profit as primary runs the risk of elevating gold—mere metal—over everything of human value. Here the discussion must go even deeper into your economic philosophy, your understanding of the purpose of work, and your beliefs about where you and your company fit into the whole world and its larger social community.

This chapter presents more issues and arguments about the larger area of corporate social responsibility (CSR) and its relationship to business and economic theory.

First we will present some of the specific arguments against the concept of CSR.

Next we will contrast the shareholder and stakeholder theories; raise the issue of the real costs of business when social and environmental factors are included, and present the idea of a "social contract" between business and society.

Then we will investigate some of the possibilities, both good and bad, for the future of CSR.

Finally, we will raise questions for reflection and a peek at what's ahead.

The CSR Debate

Not everyone thinks corporate social responsibility (CSR) is a good or even necessary movement for business. The following comments show some of the more prevalent differing viewpoints.

CSR as disguised collectivism

Milton Friedman, Nobel Prize-winning economist known for his advocacy of laissez-faire capitalism, criticizes CSR as a doctrine that believes that

> collectivist ends can be attained without collectivist means. That is why, in my book *Capitalism and Freedom*, I have called it a "fundamentally subversive doctrine" in a free society, and have said that in such a society, "there is one and only one social responsibility of business—to use its resources and engage in activities designed to increase its profits so long as it stays within the rules of the game, which is to say, engages in open and free competition without deception or fraud."[1]

CSR as unethical

One writer in *The Economist*, offers the following opinion:

> From an ethical point of view, the problem with conscientious (as opposed to fake) CSR is obvious: it is philanthropy at other people's expense. . . . Profit-maximising CSR does not silence the critics, which was the initial aim; CSR that is not profit-maximising might silence the critics but is, in fact, unethical.[2]

CSR as a delusion

Clive Crook argues that capitalism "does not need the fundamental reform that many CSR advocates wish for"[3] and that CSR
advocates are fooling themselves.

> Most CSR, in fact, is probably delusional, meaning that it
> reduces both profits and social welfare, even if the cost under
> both headings is usually small. Almost all CSR has at least
> some cost, after all, even if it is no more than a modest
> increase in the firm's bureaucratic overhead.[4]

CSR as an obligation of the powerful

On the other hand, Mark Goyder, writing for the *Ethical Corporation*, points out that power in society has shifted.

> Over centuries, power has shifted. Its source was once
> military. Then came the church, then monarchy, and now
> corporations. The more power you have, the more obligation
> there is to exercise it responsibly. Staying silent when there are
> others to tackle the issue is one thing. Staying silent on planet-
> threatening issues when no single authority exists to tackle
> those issues is a retreat from obligation and not democratic
> self-restraint.[5]

CSR as changing existing market rules

George Lakoff, professor of linguistics and cognitive science at UC
Berkeley, first demonstrates that our "free" market is free within established rules and then proposes a different perspective:

> Suppose we were to change the accounting rules, so that we
> not only had open accounting, which we really need, but we
> also had full accounting. Full accounting would include things
> like ecological accounting. You could no longer dump your stuff
> in the river or the air and not pay a fee. No more free dumping.
> If you had full accounting, that constructs the market in a
> different way. It's still a market, and it's still "free" within the
> rules. But the rules are always there. It's important . . . to get
> that idea out there, that all markets are constructed. We should

be debating how they're constructed, how they should be constructed, and how are they stacked to serve particular interests.[6]

Shareholder vs. Stakeholder Theory

Note: In these discussions, the terms *stockholder* and *shareholder* are used interchangeably.

In Chapter 8, we discussed classic economic theory, which claims that the purpose of business is to make a profit for the shareholders. Today, other theories are competing with the classic theory.

For example, stakeholder theory says that business should serve the interests of all *stakeholders*; in other words, all who are affected by the company. R. Edward Freeman speaks of the "big five" stakeholders: shareholders, employees, suppliers, customers, and communities.

Alexei M. Marcoux, assistant professor of management at Loyola University in Chicago, explains stakeholder theory this way:

> The very purpose of the firm, according to this view, is to serve and coordinate the interests of its various stakeholders. It is the moral obligation of the firm's managers to strike an appropriate balance among the big five interests in directing the activities of the firm. . . .
>
> Stakeholder theory seeks to overthrow the shareholder orientation of the firm. It is an outgrowth of the corporate social responsibility (CSR) movement. . .
>
> Stakeholder theorists . . . maintain that firms are social institutions and their managers are community leaders.[7]

On the other hand, one argument made by critics of stakeholder theory is presented this way:

> A manager told to serve two masters (a little for the equity holders, a little for the community) has been freed of both and is answerable to neither. Faced with a demand from either group, the manager can appeal to the interests of the other.[8]

Milton Friedman insists that any socially responsible decision that a corporate executive makes that does not promote profit, and profit alone, is spending someone else's money.[9]

The Real Costs of Business and Capital

One powerful argument of the proponents of CSR is that much of the profit of businesses can be claimed only by ignoring the costs that are borne by others.

> A most dramatic example: the asbestos business ceased to exist when it was finally required to pay the costs of the illnesses it created. The strange lens through which we regard business, the principle that it is an "older brother" of democracy free from any rules, usually dictates that third party costs of business activities are either officially ignored, left to rest on the affected individuals themselves, or are paid by the taxpayers. The recent hypocritical revolt by the Contract Republican Congress against unfunded mandates conveniently ignored the fact that most such mandates (forcing us to pay costs of activities we don't agree with) are imposed by business, not government.

> Like any other member of a human community, businessmen should take responsibility for their choices. The first step is to stop kidding ourselves and acknowledge all the consequences and costs of business decisions. Once we know what we are really dealing with, we can fashion ways to solve problems, or can avoid causing them in the first place. As long as we are blind, we must stumble. I am not arguing that business should be welfare, only that Western civilization took a strange misstep when it first considered that liberty was best guaranteed by allowing the owners to be more important than everyone else in the relationship.[10]

The Economist argues against the CSR concept of sustainable development and criticizes the triple bottom line. It claims that "measuring profits is fairly straightforward,"[11] but the costs and benefits of environmental protection and social justice are not measurable to the same degree of precision. In fact, there is no agreement on how to define these intangibles. Consequently, the three "bottom lines" cannot be weighted against each other, and only profits can prove the success of a business. An executive can be held accountable to a profit bottom line, but cannot easily be held accountable to progress in environmental protection or social justice.

R. Edward Freeman argues against this position:

> Shareholder value orthodoxy . . .appears to give us more precision in decision-making than there really is. Using the tools and techniques developed over the last 50 years, managers can calculate 'precise' effects on shareholder value on a project-by-project basis. . . . . [But this] ignores the effects on other stakeholders, and each assumes that executives have control over other variables, such as who finds out about these decisions . . .In today's world . . . the precision of the shareholder value model is a false hope.[12]

Freeman goes on to state:

> First of all we need to take the idea of "stakeholders", "managing for stakeholders", "stakeholder management", "stakeholder dialogue", "stakeholder capitalism", etc. very seriously. We need literally to rewrite management theory and practice so that these ideas are at the centre. We need to see the executive's job as how to get stakeholder interests to move in roughly the same direction. Of course shareholders have to win, but customers, suppliers, employees and communities have to win as well . . . .

> Second . . . we need to see business activity as a moral activity, an activity that affects the hopes and dreams and well-being of many human beings. The shareholder orthodoxy would have us believe that we can separate "business" from "ethics", but the real world tells us that we can't and shouldn't.[13]

In her book *Megatrends 2010: The Rise of Conscious Capitalism*, Patricia Aburdene identified Conscious Capitalism as one of the emerging megatrends.

> Conscious Capitalism is the dynamic matrix of social, economic and spiritual trends transforming free enterprise.[14]

In a similar vein Paul Hawken proposes that we pay attention to what he calls "Natural Capitalism."

> Everyone is familiar with the traditional definition of capital as accumulated wealth in the form of investments, factories, and equipment. "Natural capital," on the other hand, comprises the resources we use, both nonrenewable (oil, coal, metal ore) and renewable (forests, fisheries, grasslands) . . . .
>
> We don't know if our economy is growing because the indices we rely upon, such as the GDP, don't measure growth. The GDP measures money transactions on the assumption that when a dollar changes hands, economic growth occurs. But there is a world of difference between financial exchanges and growth. Compare an addition to your home to a two-month stay in the hospital for injuries you suffered during a mugging. Say both cost the same. Which is growth? The GDP makes no distinction . . . .
>
> We know the price of everything but the cost of nothing. Price is what the buyer pays. Cost is what society pays. . . . A pesticide may be priced at $35 per gallon, but what does it cost society as the pesticide makes its way into wells, rivers, and bloodstreams?[15]

The Economist concedes that the real position of CSR is to aknowledge the factors besides profit that corporations need to consider and take into account. It argues, however, that focusing narrowly on profits does not endanger the environment, does not systematically ignore the rights of workers, does not intrude on the rights of other stakeholders, and does not "fail to serve the public interest."[16]

A New Social Contract

Ian Davis, worldwide managing director of McKinsey & Company, insists that social issues are really fundamental to business and that social pressures may even be "early indicators of factors core to corporate profitability." He continues:

> Big business provides huge and critical contributions to modern society . . . . Among these are productivity gains, innovation

and research, employment, large-scale investments, human-capital development and organisation.[17]

Between shareholder and stakeholder theories, Davis offers a softer approach to the classic theory. He proposes a social contract approach to solving the debate about the role of business.

> Shareholder value should continue to be seen as the critical measure of business success. However, it may be more accurate, more motivating—and indeed more beneficial to shareholder value over the long term—to describe business's ultimate purpose as the efficient provision of goods and services that society wants.

> This is a hugely valuable, even noble, purpose. It is the fundamental basis of the contract between business and society, and forms the basis of most people's real interactions with business. CEOs could point out that profits should not be seen as an end in themselves, but rather as a signal from society that their company is succeeding in its mission of providing something people want—and doing it in a way that uses resources efficiently relative to other possible uses. From this perspective, shareholder-value creation or profits are the measure, and the reward, of success in delivering to society the more fundamental business purpose. The measures and rewards reflect the predominant values of the relevant society.[18]

The Future of CSR

What is the next direction for business ethics and specifically for corporate social responsibility in the world? Some visionaries see possibilities; some critics have a more cynical view.

In *Liberating the Corporate Soul*, Richard Barrett writes:

> All human motivations are based on self-interest. We are motivated to do something only when it benefits us in some way. What about the common good? Are actions that support the common good also based on self-interest? Yes, but the self that has the interest is a different self. It is a self that transcends selfishness. It is a self with an enlarged sense of

identity. It is a self that identifies with family, community, the organization it works for, and the planet. It is a self that recognizes that it is a part of a web of interconnectedness that links all humanity and living systems. In management terminology, it is a self with a systems perspective. In spiritual terminology, it is a self in touch with its soul.[19]

Sir Geoffery Chandler, former director of Royal Dutch/Shell Group and founder-chair of Amnesty International UK Business Group writes:

The moral argument for doing good should be reason enough for companies to behave responsibly. . . . To suggest—as the business case essentially does—that doing right needs to be justified by its economic reward is amoral, a self-inflicted wound hugely damaging to corporate reputation. . . . If we are to preserve the most effective mechanism the world has known for the provision of goods and services—that is the market economy with the public limited company its main instrument—then it has to be underpinned by principle. Financial failure can destroy individual companies. Moral failure will destroy capitalism.[20]

Has CSR been co-opted and turned into a corporate possession? *The 2003 Lifeworth Annual Review of Corporate Responsibility* proclaimed "that it is time for CSR 'to grow up or fade away.' " Dr. Jem Bendell[21] writes:

People are becoming increasingly disheartened with CSR initiatives, as they're often used to promote an ideological agenda that gets big business and government off the hook for the state of the world. Christian Aid's recent report shows that major non-governmental organizations (NGOs) are turning against CSR. It's time for CSR to grow up and address the systemic problems with globalisation, or fade away into irrelevance.[22]

Issues of concern to the *Lifeworth* reviewers included "the lobbying influence and tax-avoidance strategies of large corporations, as well as the responsibility of corporations for war and poverty."[23]

The Introduction to *The 2004 Lifeworth Annual Review of Corporate Responsibility* continues in the same vein.

Exploitative North-South supply chains, tax avoidance, and anti-competitive practices are fairly typical of international corporations, undermining their economic contribution to development. These economic issues have been overlooked by mainstream work on corporate responsibility, but this review chronicles those initiatives and debates during 2004 that together suggest such economic issues will become more central in future . . . .

We believe that the movement is at a crucial juncture. Companies have climbed the corporate social responsibility (CSR) learning curve and are now playing the game like ex-perts . . . .

The question then becomes: is CSR, as it is currently being preached and practiced by multinational corporations around the world, actually a red herring? Is it a distraction from the more fundamental transformation (perhaps revolution even) of the capitalist business model which is needed? And as CSR becomes an established professional practice, will it take as given that its purpose is to benefit those who employ its professionals, rather than a primary goal of transforming the world? If so, CSR will have contributed towards a global "Crash and Burn" scenario, with growing ecological and social degradation. [24]

Next Steps – Lifeworth

Lifeworth is launching the Transcending Leadership Study Circle in mid-2006. This is your chance to be in on the beginning. Jem Bendell explains:

Many assume that leadership is about leading people towards the goal of their employer or their group. This is a partial and bounded form of leadership, unsuited to the complex challenges of our time. We need people to transcend the boundaries around their job, community or nation, and engage others in dialogue and action to address systemic problems. We can call this 'Transcending Leadership'. It is a form of leadership that transcends a limited conception of self, as the individual leader identifies with ever-greater wholes. Ultimately, Transcending Leadership is a form of action that transcends the need for a single leader, by helping others to transcend their limited states of consciousness and concern and inspire them to also lead for the common good. . . .

Initiatives in the field of 'authentic leadership', 'transformational leadership', and 'servant leadership' all relate to aspects of the personal qualities described above. The aim of the Transcending Leadership Study Circle is to integrate insights from these different fields with a focus on global social change, and to share the learning with all who are interested in this area.

This circle is open to anyone who seeks to cultivate Transcending Leadership within their organisation or through its work, and who can contribute substantively to a process of elucidating the principles, purpose, and practices of Transcending Leadership, and how to cultivate and sustain that leadership. The project will be open source, with all intellectual outputs made freely available. One output already scheduled is a forthcoming special issue of the *Journal of Corporate Citizenship* on 'Consciousness, Leadership and Humanity.' [25]

Next Steps – Corporation 2020

Launched in Boston in May 2004, Corporation 2020 was founded on the premise that

Societal expectations and needs in the 21st century demand greater corporate focus on urgent global imperatives—economic, environmental, and social. In the face of both peril and promise for the future, it is no longer enough to ask, "What is the business case for social responsibility?" Now the question must become, "What is the social purpose case for business?"[26]

A year-long multi-stakeholder process produced the following six Principles of Corporate Redesign:[27]

1. The purpose of the corporation is to harness private interests in service to the public interest.

2. Corporations shall accrue fair returns for shareholders, but not at the expense of the legitimate interests of other stakeholders.

3. Corporations shall operate sustainably, meeting the needs of the present generation without compromising the ability of future generations to meet their needs.

4. Corporations shall distribute their wealth equitably among those who contribute to its creation.

5. Corporations shall be governed in a manner that is participatory, transparent, ethical, and accountable.

6. Corporations shall not infringe on the right of natural persons to govern themselves, nor infringe on other universal human rights.

Questions for Reflection

1. What is the purpose of business? What is the responsibility of business to the rest of society?

2. Which arguments for and against CSR are most compelling for you? Why?

3. Are you a stockholder? In what other ways are you a stakeholder in business?

4. Do you agree that a corporate executive is relieved of the responsibility of considering any motive or goal other than the profit of the company's shareholders?

Looking Ahead

Chapter 11, "The Spiritual Workplace" describes characteristics of a spiritual workplace as envisioned by several experts in the field. The chapter then presents six principles for a spiritual workplace and provides examples of some companies that have won recognition for their spirituality.

Endnotes

1   Milton Friedman, "The Social Responsibility of Business is to Increase its Profits," *The New York Times Magazine,* September 13, 1970 http://www.colorado.edu/studentgroups/libertarians/issues/friedman-soc-resp-business.html (Accessed February 28, 2006)

2   "Two-faced capitalism" Jan 22,2004. From *The Economist* print edition. http://www.economist.com/agenda/displaystory.cfm?story_id=2369912 (Accessed May 23, 2005)

3   Clive Crook, "The good company," *The Economist* print edition, Jan 20th 2005, http://www.economist.com/displaystory.cfm?story_id=3555212 (Accessed May 23, 2005)

4   "The union of concerned executives," *The Economist* print edition, Jan 20th 2005, http://www.economist.com/PrinterFriendly.cfm?Story_ID=3555194 (Accessed May 23, 2005)

5   Mark Goyder, "Why the Business of Business is more than business," Ethical Corporation, June 21, 2005, http://www.ethicalcorp.com/login.asp?mode=premium&Referrer=content%2Easp%3FContentID%3D3736 (Accessed July 15, 2005)

6   George Lakoff, in "'The 'free market' doesn't exist: More on framing from George Lakoff," an interview with the UC Berkeley News, 12 October, 1993. http://www.berkeley.edu/news/media/releases/2003/10/27_lakoff_p2.shtml (Accessed August 19, 2005)

7   Alexei M. Marcoux, assistant professor of management at Loyola University in Chicago, "Business Ethics Gone Wrong" *Cato Policy Report,* May/June 2000, Vol. XXII, No. 3. July 24, 2000.

8   Frank H. Easterbrook and Daniel Fischel, "The Economic Structure of Corporate Law" (1991), p. 38.

9   Milton Friedman, Nobel Prize-winning economist known for his advocacy of laissez-faire capitalism, "The Social Responsibility of Business is to Increase its Profits," *The New York Times Magazine,* September 13, 1970. Online at http://www.colorado.edu/studentgroups/libertarians/issues/friedman-soc-resp-business.html

10 Jonathan Wallace, "Compassionate Capitalism," *The Ethical Spectacle* – April 1997, http://www.spectacle.org/497/dem.html (Accessed May 23, 2005)

11 "The world according to CSR," *The Economist* print edition, Jan 20th 2005 http://www.economist.com/PrinterFriendly.cfm?Story_ID=3555272 (Accessed May 23, 2005)

12 R. Edward Freeman, "Foreword" in Jörg Andriof, Sandra Waddock, Bryan Husted, and Sandra Sutherland Rahman, *Unfolding Stakeholder Thinking, Vol. I: Theory, Responsibility and Engagement.* http://www.greenleaf-publishing.com/catalogue/unfold.htm#chdownload (Accessed June 17, 2005)

13 *Ibid.*

14 Aburdene, *op. cit.,* p. 45.

15 Paul Hawken, "Natural Capitalism," *Mother Jones,* March/April 1997
http://www.motherjones.com/news/feature/1997/03/hawken-2.html
(Accessed July 19, 2005)
16 "The world according to CSR," *The Economist* print edition, Jan 20th 2005
http://www.economist.com/PrinterFriendly.cfm?Story_ID=3555272 (Accessed May 23, 2005)
17 Ian Davis, "The biggest contract," *The Economist* print edition, May 26th
2005, http://www.economist.com/business/displayStory.cfm?story_id=
4008642 (Accessed February 28, 2006)
18 *Ibid.*
19 *Liberating the Corporate Soul: Building a Visionary Organization,* (1998,
Butterworth-Heinemann, now part of Elsevier), p. 40
20 Sir Geoffery Chandler, "Let's Not Fool Each Other with the Business Case,"
Institutional Shareowner. Reprinted with permission from *Ethical Performance,* May 2002 (Volume 4, Issue 1) http://www.institutional
shareowner.com/commentary.html?id=9 (Accessed June 16, 2005)
21 Teaching fellow at the University of Nottingham (UK) International Centre
for Corporate Social Responsibility; Adjunct Professor at Auckland University
of Technology, in New Zealand; UN consultant
22 http://www.new-academy.ac.uk/publications/lifeworthreviews/home.htm
(Accessed January 4, 2005) *The Lifeworth Annual Review of Corporate Responsibility* is supported by the New Academy of Business.
23 *Ibid.*
24 http://www.lifeworth.net/ (Accessed February 3, 2006)
25 http://www.transcendingleadership.net/ Accessed February 20, 2006
26   http://www.corporation2020.org/ (Accessed January 31, 2005)
27 *Ibid.*

Part IV   Living into Your
Spiritual Future
at Work

Consider your role as a spiritual leader in Chapters 11-12:

6 principles for a spiritual workplace

Examples of spiritual companies

6 human issues in leadership

Changing the cultural values at work

11 The Spiritual Workplace

THE MEANING OF PEACE

There once was a King who offered a prize to the artist who would paint the best picture of peace. Many artists tried. The King looked at all the pictures, but there were only two he really liked and he had to choose between them.

One picture was of a calm lake. The lake was a perfect mirror, for peaceful towering mountains were all around it. Overhead was a blue sky with fluffy white clouds. All who saw this picture thought that it was a perfect picture of peace.

The other picture had mountains too. But these were rugged and bare. Above was an angry sky from which rain fell and in which lightening played. Down the side of the mountain tumbled a foaming waterfall. This did not look peaceful at all. But when the King looked, he saw behind the waterfall a tiny bush growing in a crack in the rock. In the bush a mother bird had built her nest. There, in the midst of the rush of angry water, sat the mother bird on her nest... perfect peace.

The King chose the second picture.

"Because," explained the King, "peace does not mean to be in a place where there is no noise, trouble, or hard work. Peace means to be in the midst of all those things and still be calm in your heart. That is the real meaning of peace."[A]

Creating a "feel-good" environment for your employees does not make a company spiritual. In fact, it may actually help executives to cover up poor or deceptive ways of doing business.

"Improving our ethics" is not enough either. Some companies emphasize their clean accounting practices but still ignore their corporate social responsibilities. Others may do the opposite. Both the business ethics within a company's direct operation and the company's commitment to corporate social responsibility are essential parts of being a spiritual company. But that isn't all. Even if a company does both of these things well and is a very "good" company, it still may not be open to spirituality.

This chapter addresses the specifically spiritual quality that makes a good company also a spiritual, or spiritually-friendly, company.

First we will look at some characteristics of a spiritual workplace as described several professionals who have written on the subject.

Next we will discuss six basic principles for a spiritual workplace.

Then we will present examples of some specific companies that have received awards for being spiritual workplaces.

Finally, we will raise questions for reflection and take a peek at what's ahead.

Characteristics of a Spiritual Workplace

This section presents the characteristics of a spiritual workplace as described by the following professionals who have written on the subject:

- **Martin Rutte**, author of *Chicken Soup for the Soul at Work,* is a professional speaker, consultant, and president of Livelihood, a management consulting firm in Santa Fe, New Mexico. He is also Chair of the Board of the new Centre for Spirituality and the Workplace at the Sobey School of Business, Saint Mary's University, Halifax, Nova Scotia, Canada.[2]

- **Tim McGuire** is a long-time journalist who writes a weekly syndicated column for United Media called "More Than Work." His column addresses ethics, spirituality, and values in work.

- **Rick James** is a Senior Capacity Building Specialist for the International NGO[3] Training and Research Centre. He has written extensively on NGO capacity building and on organizational change issues.

- The **Association for Spirit at Work (ASAW)** founded by **Judith A. Neal,** is a non-profit association of people and organizations who are interested in the study and/or practice of spirituality in the workplace.

- **Paul T. P. Wong** is an ordained pastor, a registered clinical psychologist, and a university professor, who integrates psychology and spirituality. He is the founding Director of the Graduate Program in Counseling Psychology at Trinity Western University in British Columbia, Canada, and founding President of the International Network on Personal Meaning and the International Society for Existential Psychology and Psychotherapy.

- **The Findhorn Foundation Consultancy Service (FFCS)** does management and organizational consulting, team building and staff development. Working with the whole person, its emphasis is on experiential learning, creative methods, and drawing out the full potential of each person or group.[4]

Martin Rutte

In his article "Spirituality in the Workplace, Martin Rutte describes a spiritual workplace:

> What would a more spiritual workplace mean for people? It would mean that work would move from merely being a place to get enough money to survive—from just earning our daily bread—to being a place of **livelihood**. By livelihood I mean a place where we both survive and are fully alive. We are alive in that our spirit fully expresses itself. And through our contribution, we allow other people's spirits to be nourished and to flourish.[5]

In another article, Rutte elaborates on what he means by livelihood:

> Livelihood has three components. The first is survival. We still need to eat, we still need to have shelter, and we still need to be responsible for our families. These needs don't just vanish.

They still must be met. To put it simply, Stage 1 of livelihood is: "You're alive."

Secondly, we want our souls to be nourished and our hearts to be touched. We hunger for our work to provide us with full creative expression. Our gift, our purpose, our "vocation of destiny" longs to be both experienced and expressed. We want more than just survival. We want our aliveness to flourish. Stage 2 of livelihood is: "Your aliveness."

When you take "Your aliveness" and contribute it through your self, through your product or service—out to others, out into the world—Stage 3 of livelihood occurs: "Their aliveness."[6]

Tim McGuire

Characteristics of a spiritual workplace go beyond the legal requirements for ethical compliance. In his August 4, 2003, "More Than Work" column, Tim McGuire proposes three basic principles to consider in making your workplace spiritual:

The first is the principle that labor is more important than capital.

The second principle is that work should not only change the object of the work but should positively change the subject doing the work. That means that if the worker is building a widget the widget should become a finished quality product AND the worker should also grow and develop in the process.

The third basic principle is the most obvious, but apparently the most difficult—the golden rule. If employers and workers treated each other the way they want to be treated, much of this anger and venom would subside.[7]

The Association for Spirit at Work (ASAW)

The Association for Spirit at Work carefully defines spirituality and its meaning in the workplace:

The "vertical" component in spirituality—a desire to transcend the individual ego or personality self. . . . This dimension is experienced as a conscious sense of profound connection to the Universe/God/ Spirit. . . .

The "horizontal" component in spirituality—a desire to be of service to other humans and the planet. In the horizontal we seek to make a difference through our actions. . . .

Spirituality in the workplace means that employees find nourishment for both the vertical and horizontal dimensions of their spirituality at work.[8]

Rick James

In a publication of the Swedish Mission Council,[9] Rick James writes:

The subject of spirituality is a personal, sensitive and flammable subject. Some attempts to bring spiritual perspectives into organisation and management have been reckless, exclusive and even damaging. But the importance of the subject makes it imperative to grow in our understanding and ability to discuss the spiritual more explicitly. Spirituality, after all, is clearly not the monopoly of any one religion and is informed by a wide variety of faiths. Although the spiritual is very personal, it does not necessarily follow that it must also remain private.[10]

At the heart of the matter is the question of whether or not there is an outside spiritual force that complements, and indeed even empowers the work of the human spirit. This would make improvement more than simply self-help.[11]

In a more extensive discussion of spirituality in organizational change, James elaborates:

Spirituality is becoming part of mainstream organizational theory and practice. It is no longer viewed as the preserve of a "new age" or "fundamentalist" fringe. In the last five years management journals, conferences, academic syllabuses and popular writers have increasingly focused on the spiritual dimension to organisations and change.[12]

Although the word spirituality is defined in a variety of ways, there is a general consensus among management writers on what this looks like when applied to organisations and also to leadership. Some of the major elements that are common to most are an emphasis on:

- Vision and values
- Service and love for others
- Empowering others
- Relationships of trust
- Changing from within
- Courage to overcome fears
- A divine spark or energy

The first six of these 'spiritual' elements are generally accepted as good organizational practice. Humanists may see them as arising from our own human nature and some might be uncomfortable having the label 'spiritual' attached to them.[13]

While some assert that these are all products of the human spirit, others believe that there is a divine Spirit that is not only the source of these principles, but also empowers people and enables them to live them out. They believe that at the core of any positive human and organizational change there is a divine spark or breath of life, which comes from 'common grace'.[14]

Paul T. P. Wong

In "Spirituality and Meaning at Work," Paul T. P. Wong discusses the role of spirituality in the workplace:

Spirituality should not be used as a religious garment or a marketing tool. It is concerned with substance rather than image. More specifically, it has to do with how we define ourselves, view the world, relate to others, and make ethical/ moral decisions.

Some of the "attributes of spirituality within the context of work" that Wong lists are:

- Affirming meaning and purpose in spite of absurdity and chaos

- Recognizing the immaterial, transcendental, sacred dimensions of reality

- Having a servant's attitude towards work and leadership

- Emphasizing social responsibility toward the community, society and environment

- Viewing God and spiritual principles as the grounding for moral decisions[15]

The Findhorn Foundation Consultancy Service (FFCS)

Trainers Robin Alfred and Robin Shohet of FFCS identify five linked dimensions of spirituality, specifically spirituality at work:

1. **Working towards the realisation of the highest potential in each individual.** To do this means working from a paradigm of collaboration rather than competition. It involves seeing the potential for good in each person that we relate to, be they client, colleague, manager or competitor, and enabling each of us to be the very best that we can be. It means working from a basis of trust instead of mistrust, and seeking to support and develop one another, rather than undermine and sabotage each other's efforts. . . .

2. **Seeking to embody spiritual values (love, acceptance, compassion, forgiveness, integrity, honesty) in all that we do and in all our relationships.** This too is easier said than done. We spring so easily to judgement; hang on to grudges; take secret delight, or at least comfort, in someone else's perceived "failure"; conspire to hide the truth from our colleagues, our customers, our competitors and ourselves; and daily fail to act with full integrity. . . .

3. **Making space for all that stops us - we might call this working with the shadow, and the "inner critic" or judge.** Paradoxically, as we reach for the heights of (1.) and (2.), we need equally to plumb the depths and dig in the dirt for the tools that will help us. Failing to do so will render all our best intentions merely that—intentions. . . . examine the blocks that will stop us

from achieving all that we set out to achieve. These may be political, personal, biological—it matters not. They must be brought out into the light, and unpacked and examined or they will surely defeat us and our best efforts. . . .

An organisation that seeks to bring spirituality into its workplace will also make space for this. In terms of SWOT analysis[16], this can be seen as the focus on "Weaknesses" and "Threats" alongside "Strengths" and "Opportunities". But we need to deepen this practice and look too at our personal and relational shadows, at our inner critics and the voices in our own heads and hearts that tell us we are not good enough, that we can't do it, and that collude with our sense of inadequacy.

4. **Acting in ways that acknowledge, embrace and enhance the presence of something beyond the physical here and now, beyond that which we can perceive with our senses of touch, taste, smell, sight and hearing.** In an organisation where this dimension of spirituality is thriving and apparent, we might expect to see a willingness to live in the realm of chaos and uncertainty in place of the known, familiar and expected; an honouring of the intuitive and of "hunches" in place of rule-governed behaviour where everything needs to be justified in terms of pre-set criteria. . . . We might, above all, feel the presence of mystery and surprise, and relish the joy of spontaneity and the wonder of paradox.

5. **Understanding the holographic principle.** The holographic principle is an invitation to see the world as deeply interconnected and to understand reality as comprising nests of holograms. When an issue arises in my work I can choose to look at it as if through a microscope—what exactly is going on with this issue? And that can be helpful. I can, however, also choose to look at it from a "macroscopic" perspective. How is this problem a reflection of bigger problems in the company? How might these in turn be connected to wider issues in society and in the world? Seeing my life and my work as taking place within a multi-layered hologram, where the seeds and blueprint at one level are present in the next and also in the previous, gives me far greater perspective.[17]

Six Principles for a Spiritual Workplace

The following sections present six principles that I believe are essential to creating a spiritual workplace.

The Principle of a Meaningful Purpose

Clearly the purpose of business must be greater than making the most profit possible for investors. There isn't any view of spirituality that values money above everything else. Even without trying to be a spiritual company, business leaders can set higher aspirations than profit alone. David Packard, co-founder of Hewlett-Packard™ Company, says:

> Many people assume, wrongly, that a company exists solely to make money. People get together and exist as a company so that they are able to accomplish something collectively that they could not accomplish separately—they make contributions to society.[18]

> To be useful an invention must not only fill a need, it must be an economical and efficient solution to that need.[19]

McGuire emphasizes "labor over capital" as a basic characteristic of a spiritual workplace. James offers "vision and values" as well as "service and love for others," while Wong says that the culture change in becoming a spiritual organization results in a business that is "purpose-driven and meaning-based."

The model of a business that is becoming spiritual moves from ownership to stewardship philosophy. Not only is labor more important than capital, but caring for the earth and preserving resources for future generations become more important than short-term profits.

> Corporate stewardship reflects a philosophy that emphasizes the proper use and allocation of a company's resources and unites its ethical values and economic mission.[20]

The Principle of Valuing People

People are ends in themselves, not a means to an end. All employees are valued and respected as human beings, not as "resources" to be used by managers. They are workers, not just "labor." They are given meaningful work that contributes to society. Their input is sought and their creativity is encouraged. Corporate values and ethics are communicated and discussed with them, and whistle-blowers are protected. Diversity of all kinds is not only tolerated but sought.

A Northwestern University study has shown a direct link between employee satisfaction and customer satisfaction and from there to better financial performance.[21]

The workplace becomes, in Rutte's words, "a place of livelihood where . . . spirit fully expresses itself and is nourished."

The same principle applies to contractors, suppliers, and customers. Whatever the economic transaction, they are not to be exploited. Even decisions regarding global trade and outsourcing must be made with this principle in mind.

The Principle of Intentional Service

The products and/or services provided by the business fill a real need. Profit is the reward, not the purpose, of the business. McGuire points to the Golden Rule, and Wong emphasizes servanthood and social responsibility.

Neal and ASAW describe the horizontal aspect of spirituality as service and action. The application for the International Spirit at Work Award describes the "horizontal" component in spirituality as

> a desire to be of service to other humans and the planet. In the horizontal we seek to make a difference through our actions. This dimension is manifested externally. A person with a strong "vertical connection" who is also able to demonstrate the "horizontal dimension" has a clear grasp on his/her mission, ethics, values. A strong "horizontal" component is demonstrated by a service orientation, compassion, and a well-aligned vision/mission and values that are carried out in productive effective services and products. . . . Companies with a strong

sense of the horizontal will generally demonstrate some or all of the following:

- Caring behaviors among co-workers;
- A social responsibility orientation;
- Strong service commitments to customers;
- Environmental sensitivity;
- And a significant volume of community service activities.[22]

The Principle of Cherishing Connections

The Great Law of the Iroquois Confederacy states:

> In our every deliberation, we must consider the impact of our decisions on the next seven generations.

Wong talks about "emphasizing social responsibility toward the community, society and environment." Neal and ASAW mention environmental sensitivity as one of the indications that a company has a strong horizontal component of spirituality. FFCS trainers refer to the holographic principle.

Recognizing, cherishing, and protecting our connectedness and interdependency—both individually and as a company—in the whole of society and of the universe is crucial to being a spiritual company.

The Principle of Recognizing Mystery

James describes this Mystery as "an outside spiritual force that complements, and indeed even empowers the work of the human spirit"[23] and as "a divine Spirit that is not only the source of these principles, but also empowers people and enables them to live them out."[24]

Wong speaks of the need to recognize "the immaterial, transcendental, sacred dimensions of reality." Neal and ASAW define this vertical component of spirituality as "a conscious sense of profound connection to the Universe/God/Spirit." Further explanation is in the application for the International Spirit at Work Award. This award is

> given to selected organizations that have implemented specific policies, programs, or practices that explicitly nurture spirituality inside their organizations. . . . "Explicitly spiritual" means that the topic of spirituality is openly discussed—not just assumed or implied.[25]

The application describes the "vertical" component in spirituality as

> a desire to transcend the individual ego or personality self. The name you put on the vertical component might be God, Spirit, Universe, Higher Power or something else. There are a great many names for this vertical dimension. This dimension is experienced as a conscious sense of profound connection to the Universe/God/Spirit. This might be experienced internally as moments of awe or peak experiences. A strong, sustained vertical component reflects in outer behaviors as a person (or group) who is centered and able to tap into deep inner strength and wisdom. Generally quiet time, time in nature, or other reflective activities or practices are required to access the "vertical" component of our spirituality. . . . Examples of vertical organizational spirituality include:
>
> • Meditation time at the beginning of meetings,
>
> • Retreat or spiritual training time set aside for employees,
>
> • Appropriate accommodation of employee prayer practices,
>
> • And openly asking questions to test if company actions are aligned with higher meaning and purpose. [26]

Because diversity is not only tolerated but celebrated, employees in a spiritual or spiritually-friendly workplace feel comfortable expressing their spirituality in ways that respect and honor the differences of others. Expressions of spirituality are encouraged and faith-based groups have the same privileges and requirements as other affinity groups that are not related to work.

> Though companies could completely divorce themselves from anything to do with religion, many say that the faith-based employee resource groups complement their workforce-diversity goals and contribute to the bottom line through employee recruitment, development and retention. In addition, at least

one company believes that its willingness to confront thorny issues impresses its customers, enhancing the company's position in the marketplace.[27]

Recognizing that spirituality and spiritual principles are the basis for ethical decisions, the spiritual workplace invites employees to express their ethical values and concerns. Employees are also encouraged to name the religion, faith, or spiritual foundation from which their values and concerns come.

Whistleblowers are protected, not penalized.

The corporate vision and ethics support these basic spiritual principles. The corporate vision, values, and ethics are communicated, understood, shared, and supported, engendering trust among all the people in the company.

The Principle of Integration

Yoga classes. . . . Creativity. . . . Mindfulness. These are popular terms for company efforts at becoming spiritual without talking about it. This approach focuses only on the individual and personal aspects of spirituality.

Team-building. . . . Softball tournaments. . . . Motivational films. These are popular ways of building community and corporate loyalty without modifying the corporate structure. This approach focuses only on increasing employee satisfaction and productivity.

Posting corporate codes of ethics. . . . Recycling. . . . Corporate donations to major disaster relief. These are popular attempts at building a corporate reputation without changing the corporate values. They demonstrate corporate social concern in ways that provide the greatest public relations value with the least inner change or commitment.

Becoming a spiritual workplace also requires a culture change. It requires addressing all of the issues mentioned in this book–treatment of all the workers at all levels of the company, business philosophy, internal ethics, corporate social responsibility and explicit recognition of the spiritual aspect of life–while remaining well-managed financially. As the application for the International Spirit at Work Award puts it:

> Spirituality in the workplace means that employees find nourishment for both the vertical and horizontal dimensions of their spirituality at work. . . .The vertical and horizontal dimensions should be well integrated—so that motivations (sourced from the vertical) and actions (horizontal manifestations) are explicitly linked.[28]

The FFCS suggests the addition of a fourth bottom line to the triple bottom line of economic, social, and environmental performance:

> We would add a fourth criterion, and suggest that the successful business of the 21st century will need to be **spiritually intelligent** as well. It will need to understand its purpose in the world and be able to translate that into meaningful work for its staff. It will seek to operate by spiritual, as well as economic, environmental and social values. It will live more comfortably on the edge of chaos, welcoming paradox and uncertainty, intuition and creativity, collaboration and cooperation.
>
> Above all it will see itself as simply one part of the huge web of interconnectedness that makes up our planet, striving to be in right relationship with all of its parts, and playing its own unique and humble role in the evolution of society.[29]

The Principle of Integration is this "fourth bottom line."

Examples of Spiritual Companies

The companies described in this section are among those that have been honored for their excellence in one of the areas discussed in this chapter. The award criteria used by the groups that honored these companies are listed in Appendix A.

Men's Wearhouse™

The Men's Wearhouse, Inc.[30] has made *Fortune's* list of "100 Best Companies to Work for in America" for several years. It began changing its corporate culture more than a dozen years ago and made employee fulfillment its first priority, followed by the well-being of other stakeholders. Its website includes many pages dealing with its philosophy and encouraging further communication both with its employees and the public.

The mission of Men's Wearhouse, as stated on its website, is:

> To maximize sales, provide value to our customers and deliver top quality customer service while still having fun and maintaining our values.
>
> These values include nurturing creativity, growing together, admitting to mistakes, promoting a happy and healthy lifestyle, enhancing a sense of community and striving toward becoming self-actualized people.[31]

George Zimmer, founder and CEO, writes:

> But bottom line, our success depended on the quality of the relationships we had with our stakeholders: customers, vendors, shareholders, and the communities in which we did business.
>
> I further realized that lasting relationships need to be grounded in trust. In our case, trust was built on personal interactions: . . .
>
> We discovered that the quality of trust we built with the people who came through our doors depended on how well we trusted those we worked with. Our "outer" relationships were driven by the quality of our "inner" work environment. So our collective honesty, sincerity, integrity, responsiveness, authenticity, mutual good will, and caring for each other became my focus as CEO. . . .
>
> That's why, early on, our company became a laboratory for learning ways to teach and inspire one another. We learned the importance of establishing trusting relationships with each other and with our other stake-holders. . . .
>
> We believe that unleashing the human potential within companies, organizations, communities, and families is good for every one of us. We all have a responsibility to contribute to the extended global society to which we all belong. You might say it's our common cause.[32]

Founded in 1973, Men's Wearhouse is one of North America's largest specialty retailers of men's apparel with 689 stores and 13,200 employees.

HomeBanc Mortgage Corporation of Atlanta

HomeBanc Mortgage Corporation of Atlanta made *Fortune's* list for the first time in 2004 and made the list again in 2005. The company vision is "To become America's most admired company." Their corporate mission is "To enrich and fulfill lives by serving each other, our customers, communities and shareholders. . . as we support the dream of home ownership."

To achieve its, vision, HomeBanc's priorities are:

- Associate satisfaction
- Customer satisfaction
- Market share
- Net income

We believe that associate satisfaction drives customer satisfaction, which in turn creates market share and increases net income. Putting our Associates first is key to our success. [33]

HomeBanc also has a Faith-Based Statement which states:

As a faith-based company, HomeBanc Mortgage Corp-oration believes that associates should not have to check their spirituality at the door. We recognize that spirituality is deeply personal—we do not seek to impose any particular faith or doctrine upon any associate. We welcome people of all different beliefs into our family, treating each associate with dignity and respect. Regardless of our differences, we all share the common commitment to putting the needs of others ahead of our own. By serving others with the heart of a servant, we strive to enrich and fulfill the lives of our associates, our customers and our communities. [34]

Some of the less common employee benefits are:

an "Associate Emergency Fund," which is funded by the company's employees and designed especially for employees facing extraordinary needs such as unexpected medical bills, emergency travel expenses or other unforeseen circumstances. The company also offers a Corporate Chaplain in each region who is available to employees for funerals, weddings, counseling and other personal and professional matters.[35]

In 1994, HomeBanc was a small Atlanta-based mortgage company with about 150 employees, only one office outside the state of Georgia, and mortgage volume of about $500 million. From 1998-2002, it was first in the Atlanta area in mortgage lending. By the end of 2003, HomeBanc had about 1,300 employees in three states and closed about $6 billion in mortgage loans.

In 2004, HomeBanc Corp. became a Georgia corporation to become the parent holding company of HomeBanc Mortgage Corporation (HBMC).[36]

Sounds True

One of the 2003 recipients of the annual International Spirit at Work Award[37] is a little company in Colorado called **Sounds True**, an audio, video and music publishing company started in 1985 by Tami Simon. It describes itself this way:

From our first day in business, the Sounds True mission has been to disseminate spiritual wisdom. In a sense, we serve as an interfaith university that embraces the world's major spiritual traditions and the arts and humanities, as embodied by the leading authors, teachers, and experts of our times. Through their voices, we offer you the opportunity to pursue a lifetime of learning.[38]

In describing their work environment, Sounds True states:

We are experimenting with the creation of a unique business culture. We are dedicated to the quality, efficiency, productivity, and profitability of our work. And, we are equally dedicated to enjoying the process of the work itself, aware of the opportunity that exists at work for celebration, personal growth, and the acknowledgment of the everyday sacred.[39]

According to the award they received:

> **Sounds True's** specific practices include a contemplative dimension in the workplace through a meditation room, group meditation sessions and beginning all meetings with a minute of silence so that participants can become more present and focused on the intention of the meeting. Sounds True refers to its workplace as a "sangha"—a community of spiritual practitioners. . . . Employees can take Personal Days to attend retreats or pursue other spiritual interests. Sounds True practices open book management in order to foster trust and honesty in the workplace.[40]

The web page describing Sound True's work environment, revised in February, 2005, lists the following core values:[41]

- Multiple Bottom Lines

- A Workplace That Encourages Authenticity

  We celebrate the human experience and we welcome our whole, authentic selves into the workplace. Families, animal companions, spiritual practices, individual work styles, the lack of a dress code, and flexible schedules (when possible) are part of our culture. We honor diversity, and we are determined that no one will be disrespected on the basis of race, creed, religion, age, physical ability, or sexual orientation.

- Individual Growth and Expression

  We encourage the practice of mindfulness in every aspect of our work, fostering an atmosphere of personal responsibility and interconnectedness. We acknowledge that every person in the organization carries wisdom, and we welcome new ideas, suggestions, and perspectives, regardless of authority or position. By offering financial support for training and education, we nurture professional and personal growth.

- Building Workplace Community

  through all-company meetings, rituals, and celebrations, and by providing common gathering space. . . .

- Honest and Respectful Communication

> Conscious, mindful, direct communication and deep listen-
> ing are the foundation of our personal and group inter-
> actions. We relate to customers, vendors, professional
> partners, and each other with integrity and respect. We
> treat other people the way we would like to be treated.

- Employee Ownership

- Compassion in Action

A research team for the Center for Contemplative Mind spent two full work days at Sounds True in June, 2003. One of the themes that was evident in their time there was diversity.

> It became clear that [the employees] were referring to the
> underlying principle that seems to make Sounds True a
> rewarding workplace for most people: they feel encouraged to
> come to work and "show up as all of who they are" (a phrase
> used by a number of people we interviewed). This holds true for
> the Buddhist meditator as much as for the company's "resident
> Republican." There's a healthy sense of humor . . . most people
> don't hold the idea of spirituality too seriously, which seems to
> allow room for those at all places of the spiritual spectrum to
> be themselves. . . . The bottom line . . . . as far as employees
> are concerned, is respect for each other.[42]

The report quotes an unidentified employee:

> That's the thing that allows me to be spiritual. It's not like, "You
> can be spiritual here."' It's "bring your full self to work" and I'm
> a spiritual being. It's an outgrowth of that intention, of wanting
> people to be who they are here. That let's you off the hook of
> saying that you're "spiritual" or "contemplative" or whatever. It
> just says, "We allow for that by allowing our employees to be
> authentic."[43]

Another employee remarked:

> It's not easy to be mindful all the time. . . . It's easier to hide
> out and not be challenged, like in my old job. It was easier to
> get mad and go home and be mad at people and not like them,
> because then I didn't have to be engaged with them. I didn't
> have to go up and say what was bothering me about the

relationship, or apologize. So it really calls you to be a more mindful and better human being.[44]

Like many companies, whether or not they attempt to be spiritual, Sounds True went through a crisis when it grew faster than its organizational structure could handle. The result was a large layoff in the year 2000.

This period of learning and humility resulted in some important lessons: there's no substitute for good business practices and skills, like financial planning, management, and tracking; and being a spiritual person is no guarantee of success. In fact, employees observed, sometimes contemplative or spiritual rhetoric can be an excuse for not dealing with the nuts and bolts of running a business, like having an effective budget. From that lesson has come a reframing of the role of business and financial practices in the company, with many of the employees that we interviewed considering awareness of the company's financial goals as a kind of mindfulness practice.[45]

During this business crisis, founder and CEO Tami Simon admitted she had made some poor decisions that had helped bring about the crisis. Her humility and willingness to own her mistakes set an example for the whole company.

Sounds True has grown from one person (Tami Simon, founder and CEO) in a single room to a 55-person organization with a state-of-the-art recording and editing studio, expanded customer service capabilities, and a 10,000 square-foot warehouse.[46]

Questions for Reflection

1. What is the difference between an ethical workplace, a socially responsible workplace, and a spiritual workplace? Why should we care?

2. How does Rutte's concept of livelihood enrich your understanding of workplace spirituality?

3. Is it realistic to believe, with McGuire, that everyone's work could change the worker? Can you think of a job that needs to

be performed that, in your opinion, could not help the worker to grow? Can you find someone who does that job and inquire?

4. How do you feel about recognizing the vertical component of spirituality in the workplace as described by Neal and ASAW? Does your workplace nourish your "conscious sense of profound connection to the Universe/God/Spirit"? Does it nourish your co-workers and employees?

5. Have you witnessed the kinds of "reckless, exclusive and even damaging" spiritual perspectives referred to by James? Should we keep work and spirituality separate to prevent this kind of damage?

6. Wong says that spirituality "has to do with how we define ourselves, view the world, related to others, and make ethical/moral decisions." Can a company define itself as good, treat its employees well, and make ethical and moral and social decisions without being spiritual? What would it add to "view God and spiritual principles as the grounding for moral decisions" as Wong advocates?

7. FFCS adds the dimension of "making space for all that stops us. . . working with the shadow, and the 'inner critic' or judge." Is this really essential to success?

8. Review the Six Principles for a Spiritual Workplace. Do you consider any of the principles unnecessary? Are there others you would add?

Looking Ahead

This book is targeted at "business leaders," not just managers. Chapter 12 is titled "Integrating Spirituality into Management Practice" but the discussion there is applicable to any worker. Not all of us have management responsibility, but all of us are, or can be, spiritual leaders.

Endnotes

1 Posted on The Story Bin http://www.storybin.com/builders/builders123.shtml (Accessed September 18, 2005)
2 The Centre for Spirituality and the Workplace (established in 2004) is the first academic-based centre for spirituality and work in Canada. Its mission is to be a centre for academic activities and a centre of influence in the community, the nation and the world. http://www.spiritualityandthe workplace.ca
3 The World Bank defines NGOs as "private organizations that pursue activities to relieve suffering, promote the interests of the poor, protect the environment, provide basic social services, or undertake community development" (Operational Directive 14.70). In wider usage, the term NGO can be applied to any non-profit organization which is independent from government. Source: "Public Documents and Maps" at Duke Univeristy's Perkins Library, http://docs.lib.duke.edu/igo/guides/ngo/define.htm (Accessed March 30, 2006)
4 http://www.findhorn.org/connect/consultancy_new.php. The Findhorn Foundation is a major international centre of spiritual education and personal transformation offering many ways for people to visit, live or work here, . . . located in northeast Scotland. . . . The Findhorn Foundation is associated with the Department of Public Information of the United Nations as a Non-Governmental Organisation and is represented at regular briefing sessions at UN Headquarters. (Accessed September 22, 2005)
5 Martin Rutte, "Spirituality in the Workplace," ©1996 http://www.martinrutte.com/heart.html (Accessed September 18, 2005)
6 Martin Rutte, "Livelihood: The New context of Work," ©1996 http://www.martinrutte.com/livelihood.html (Accessed September 18, 2005)
7 "More Than Work" column for August 4, 2003, Copyright 2005, More than Work Distributed by United Feature Syndicate, Inc. http://www.timjmcguire.com/columns_output.asp?columnID=2 (Accessed January 3, 2005)
8 http://www.spiritatwork.org/awards/willisharman/whatis.htm (Accessed September 7, 2005)
9 The Swedish Mission Council is a forum for reflection about mission and the responsibility for the Churches and the Christian agencies with regard to international solidarity. The SMC is an association of 34 Swedish denominations, mission organisations and other Christian agencies.
10 Rick James, "Reflections on Current Thinking on Spirituality in Organisations" © copyright 2004 Swedish Mission Council, http://www.missioncouncil.se/publikationer/skrifter/04_1_reflections.pdf p. 5 (Accessed September 1, 2005)
11 *Ibid.,* p. 16
12 Rick James, *Creating Space for Grace: God's Power in Organisational Change* © copyright 2004 Swedish Mission Council, p. 10 http://www.missioncouncil.se/publikationer/skrifter/04_02_space_for_grace.pdf (Accessed September 1, 2005)
13 *Ibid.,* p. 15.

14 *Ibid.*, p. 19.
15 Paul T. P. Wong, "Spirituality and Meaning at Work," September, 2003. http://www.meaning.ca/articles/presidents_column/spirituality_work_sept03.htm, (Accessed September 1, 2005)
16 SWOT analysis looks at a business's internal **S**trengths and **W**eaknesses and its external **O**pportunities and **T**hreats.
17 Robin Alfred with Robin Shohet, "Developing Practical Spirituality in the Workplace," Paper for the 'Living Spirit' Conference, University of Surrey, Guildford, England, July 22-24 2002 http://www.findhorn.org/connect/cons_livingspiritpaper_new.php (Accessed August 27, 2005)
18 In a speech to employees of Hewlett-Packard, http://www.att.sbresources.com/SBR_template.cfm?document=steve.cfm&article=2004Dec06 (Accessed September 19, 2005)
19 Dave Packard, *The HP WAY—How Bill Hewlett And I Built Our Company* (NY: Harper-Collins) 1995, and http://www.bioheartinc.com/publications/newsletters/newsletter_0895d.htm (Accessed September 19, 2005)
20 http://www.commerce.gov/opa/press/Secretary_Evans/2003_Releases/June/18_Evans_CorpStewardAward.htm (Accessed September 7, 2005)
21 The Forum for People Performance Management & Measurement of North-western University, "Linking Organizational Characteristics to Employee Attitudes and Behavior—A Look at the Downstream Effects on Market Response & Financial Performance," http://www.performanceforum.org/PFM/pdf/linking_org_characteristics_to_employee_attitudes_and_behavior.pdf, p. 1 (Accessed September 22, 2005)
22 "Application for the 2006 International Spirit at Work Award," http://www.spiritatwork.org/awards/willisharman/ISAWAPPLICATION-2006.pdf (Accessed February 27, 2005)
23 Rick James, "Reflections on Current Thinking on Spirituality in Organisations" © copyright 2004 Swedish Mission Council, http://www.missioncouncil.se/publikationer/skrifter/04_1_reflections.pdf pp. 5, 16. (Accessed September 1, 2005)
24 Rick James, *Creating Space for Grace: God's Power in Organisational Change,* p. 19
25 "Application for the 2006 International Spirit at Work Award" http://www.spiritatwork.org/awards/willisharman/ISAWAPPLICATION-2006.pdf (Accessed February 27, 2006)
26 *Ibid.*
27 Todd Henneman, "A New Approach to Faith at Work" *Workforce Management*, October 2004, pp. 76-77, http://www.workforce.com/archive/feature/23/85/42/index.php (Accessed October, 2004)
28 "Application for the 2006 International Spirit at Work Award," http://www.spiritatwork.org/awards/willisharman/ISAWAPPLICATION-2006.pdf (Accessed February 27, 2006)
29 Robin Alfred with Robin Shohet, *op. cit.*
30 http://www.menswearhouse.com/home_page/ho10_home.jsp (Accessed January 4, 2005)

31 http://www.menswearhouse.com/home_page/our_company/co60_ company.jsp?FOLDER%3C%3Efolder_id=2534374302068547& bmUID=1126743740703 (Accessed September 14, 2005)

32 http://www.menswearhouse.com/home_page/common_threads/ct51_ our_philosophy.jsp?FOLDER%3C%3Efolder_id=2534374302068547& bmUID=1126744595518 (Accessed September 14, 2005)

33 http://www.homebanc.com/Careers/ValuesMissionVision.aspx (Accessed February 27, 2006)

34 http://www.homebanc.com/Careers/Careers_OurFaithBased.aspx (Accessed February 23, 2005)

35 http://www.homebanc.com/AboutHomeBanc/PressReleases/ Atlanta_Fortune100_Listing_2005.pdf (Accessed September 14, 2005)

36 http://www.homebanc.com/AboutHomeBanc/History.aspx (Accessed February 23, 2005)

37 The annual International Spirit at Work Award is given cooperatively by The Association for Spirit at Work (www.spiritatwork.org); the Spirit in Business Institute (www.spiritinbusiness.org); The World Business Academy (www.worldbusiness.org) and the European Baha'i Business Forum (www.ebbf.org)

38 http://www.soundstrue.com/aboutus.html (Accessed February 23, 2005)

39 http://www.soundstrue.com/wl_environment.html (Accessed February 23, 2005)

40 http://www.spiritatwork.org/awards/willisharman/2003announcement.html (Accessed February 23, 2005)

41 http://www.soundstrue.com/wl_environment.html (Accessed September 15, 2005)

42 "Creating the Contemplative Organization: Lessons from the Field" by Maia Duerr for The Center for Contemplative Mind in Society, p. 39-39, http://www.contemplativemind.org/programs/cnet/contorgs.pdf (Accessed September 15, 2005)

43 Ibid., p. 39

44 Ibid., p. 40

45 Ibid., p. 41-42

46 http://www.soundstrue.com/historymission.html (Accessed September 15, 2005)

12 Integrating Spirituality into Leadership and Management

FIVE MONKEYS

Five monkeys were put in the same cage. Hanging from the ceiling of the cage was a bunch of bananas. Naturally, the monkeys tried to reach for the fruit. But each time a monkey jumped to grab the bananas, a water sprinkler was turned on and water would be splashed all over the cage. The monkeys got wet, and they didn't like it. After many attempts, the monkeys stopped trying to reach for the bananas.

Then one of the five monkeys was replaced by a new monkey. The unsuspecting newcomer saw the bunch of bananas and started to reach for it. But before he could even jump, the other monkeys held him back and chattered at him loudly to avoid the spray of water. After several attempts and the same reaction from the other monkeys, the newcomer stopped trying.

A couple of days later, another one of the original monkeys was replaced. When the new monkey tried to jump for the bananas, the other four monkeys, including the one who had never been sprayed with water, all held him back and chattered at him loudly. He, too, soon stopped trying.

One by one, all of the original monkeys were replaced by new monkeys. And one by one, each of the five new monkeys stopped trying to reach the bananas, just like the original monkeys. But none of the new monkeys had ever been sprinkled with water.

The new monkeys had all learned to believe that reaching for the bananas was a bad idea and they would teach that belief to other new monkeys: Never try to get the bananas or bad things will happen to you.

ﹺﹻﹺﹻﹺﹻﹺﹻﹺﹻﹺﹻﹺﹻﹺﹻﹺﹻﹺﹻﹺﹻﹺﹻﹺﹻﹺﹻﹺﹻﹺﹻﹺﹻﹺﹻﹺﹻ

For generations we have been told to keep religion, faith, and spirituality out of business. This belief became part of our mindset. As indicated in the first chapters of this book, this mindset is changing. We don't have to be like the monkeys who have given up jumping for the bananas. We no longer have to leave our spirituality at home.

Richard Rohr says "Everything worthwhile begins with a spiritual encounter and ends in a social encounter."[1] On the other hand, making the changes in ourselves and in our corporate cultures is not an easy task.

This chapter weaves together many of the threads explored in previous chapters: the essential traits and specific on-the-job behaviors of a spiritual person, our role in business ethics and social responsibility, and our influence as leaders, whether or not we are managers.

First we will clarify some distinctions between managing and leading, keeping in mind that both functions are needed in a business organization.

Then we will explore the positive and negative aspects of six human issues that affect our spiritual leadership qualities. Each issue raises a personal question to ponder. These qualities can both help and hinder us in becoming spiritual leaders or managers.

Next we will talk about some of the changes in cultural values that are needed for a workplace to become spiritually friendly.

We will conclude with questions for reflection and look ahead to the future of the Workplace Spirituality movement.

The Functions of Managers and Leaders

Anyone in an organization can function as a leader at times. Some very good managers may find it difficult to be good leaders. Both managers and leaders are needed. This section discusses some of the differences between managing and leading.

You may be a business leader without being in management. If you are not a manager, I hope this chapter will inspire you to be a spiritual leader anyway. If you are quite comfortable as a manager, I hope the chapter will help you see the importance of management while encouraging you to develop the spiritual traits that will enable you to be a leader, too.

The roles and predominance of management and leadership vary in the workplace according to the situation, but both functions are needed. The Small Business Administration (SBA) article "Leading vs. Managing—They're Two Different Animals" offers the following contrasts:

> Managers are very good at maintaining the status quo and adding stability and order to our culture. However, they may not be as good at instigating change and envisioning the future. On the other hand, leaders are very good at stirring people's emotions, raising their expectations, and taking them in new directions (both good and bad).[2]

Traditional managers have focused on goals, problem-solving, and organizational structure and culture. The SBA article describes managers as "persistent, tough-minded, hard working, intelligent, analytical, tolerant," and leaders as "imaginative, passionate, non-conforming risk-takers."

Other relevant differences the article sets forth are:

> **Managers**. . . see themselves as conservators and regulators of an existing order of affairs with which they personally identify and from which they gain rewards; report that their role harmonizes with their ideals of responsibility and duty; perpetuate and strengthen existing institutions; display a life development process which focuses on socialization . . . this socialization process prepares them to guide institutions and to maintain the existing balance of social relations.

> **Leaders**. . . may work in organizations, but they never belong to them; report that their sense of self is independent of work roles, memberships, or other social indicators of social identity; seek opportunities for change (i.e. technological, political, or

ideological); support change; find their purpose is to profoundly alter human, economic, and political relation-ships; display a life development process which focuses on personal mastery . . . .This process impels them to struggle for psychological and social change.[3]

John P. Kotter summarizes the differences very well:

Leadership and management are two distinctive and complementary systems of action. . . .Management is about coping with complexity. Leadership, by contrast, is about coping with change.[4]

Six Human Issues in Becoming a Spiritual Leader or Manager

You have influence at work, whether it is because you are in management or because it is communicated through your personal leadership. As a manager or leader, you have significant control over the conditions under which other people must work. Your influence can be enlightening, encouraging people to grow personally and contribute productively. On the other hand, your influence can be burdensome to others if you are unaware of your own deficiencies and weaknesses and project them onto others.

The following sections present six human issues, common to all of us, that can help or hinder you in becoming a spiritual leader at work. These issues include questions to ask yourself.

Knowing Yourself

Do you know who you are? How closely is your sense of yourself tied to your job? Are you secure in your sense of self-worth apart from your work? Who are you, really?

If you are insecure in your own *identity and self-worth,* you are likely to put others down, even without realizing it, in an unconscious effort to build up your own self-esteem. Thus your leadership can be harmful to employees, colleagues and competitors. Your leadership can cause your organization to deprive its members of *their* identity and self-worth, too.

If you find meaning only in your role at work, your attitude may be destructive not only to you but to those with whom you work. It can lead them, too, to depend totally on their work for their sense of self. If they take on your compulsiveness, it is easier for you to avoid dealing with your own fears of unworthiness.

The *power* you have as a spiritual leader comes from within, but you may also have received organizational power as a supervisor, manager, or chief executive. A leader whose power comes from within is able to empower those who work for him or her. Organizational power that rests with an executive or manager is delegated to others in the lower hierarchy of the organization.

Responsibility comes along with power, both for the manager and the worker to whom organizational power is delegated. When a manager delegates power and responsibility, that manager also retains them both.

Jonathan Wallace explains:

> Whatever is delegated is still retained. If I argue I am not retaining any responsibility, than I am claiming to have abdicated power, not delegated it.
>
> . . . . An executive's statement blaming his subordinates may be translated as: "I am not a leader." [5]

Authority enables a person to make decisions without seeking permission from someone else. The person is given the power to make those independent decisions and is also given the responsibility for those decisions. He or she is held *accountable* for the results of the decisions.

Wallace continues in his discussion of traditional management process:

> Unlike responsibility, which should be as fully distributed as possible, authority must be more sparingly handed out. . . . In . . . most businesses, [the organization's vision] is imparted from the top and people join the organization based in part on their desire to adhere to the vision. . . .

> Delegating accountability unmatched by the ability to make decisions places unbearable stress on people and is also unfair. Therefore, authority and responsibility must be carefully tailored to one another. . . .
>
> While responsibility unhinged from authority creates hapless victims, authority without responsibility creates monsters. People who can make decisions for which they can never be held accountable have the potential to be incredibly destructive of the organization and of the lives of its members.[6]

A positive sense of self-worth, independent of your work, enables you to be humble in a way that you can never afford to be if you depend on your job or position to feel valuable. That kind of dependency leads to vanity, not humility. To prop up your sagging self-esteem, you will be tempted to reason that you are good and important *because* you hold a management or leadership position. This, according to Wallace, leads to vanity:

> *Vanity* is the biggest danger for all human enterprises. It is very easy to reason in reverse, from position to talent: I hold this job, therefore I am good. . . .
>
> *Humility* involves constantly reminding yourself that you do not know all the answers and that a dialog with everyone in the group offers both procedural and substantive benefits. Procedurally, the dialog communicates to the others that they are significant participants in the enterprise, with power and influence of their own. Substantively, you will learn things and be alerted to dangers you will not see on your own.
>
> The criterion for a healthy organization is not that there be no dissent, but that the dissenters trust you, and the group enough, to go along with most decisions with which they do not agree. If people hold themselves out, there is no organization.[7]

For further reflection, it may be helpful to review discussions of authenticity on page 49 and authentic behaviors on page 64, and review the discussions of humility on page 51 and humble behaviors on page 67.

Trusting the Universe

Is the universe friendly? Closely related to your identity and sense of self-worth is your ability to trust the universe (reality, God). Do you feel that you have to fight for everything, that you *must win* every competition, both in business and in your personal life, and that life itself is a battle?

If the friendliness of the universe depends on your being very good at what you do, then the fear of failure can lead to excessive anxiety and excessive activity. But that fear of failure is a fear of being imperfect—of being human—and of being deprived or punished for that imperfection. That fear often results in excessive anxiety and excessive activity. A leader or manager with this kind of anxiety demands perfection of others, too. This kind of fear is based on the illusion that *this time* we, and they, *can and must* do it perfectly!

On the other hand, some religious expressions and many self-help books and motivational speakers encourage us to believe that we deserve to be wealthy—to "make it big." If we just believe, whether in God or in ourselves, we will be rewarded. According to this teaching, the universe itself wants us to be prosperous, successful, and rich. Sometimes this message is referred to as the "prosperity gospel." However, this teaching, often accompanied by the twin promise of "feeling good," is not limited to televangelists but is also preached by many popular secular motivational speakers who promise "abundance." The unfortunate implication is that if you are *not* wealthy, then you are not good enough or you are not among the chosen. And so it becomes a position of blaming the victim.

Whatever the cause, this lack of trust leads to increased competition among individuals and between businesses. Instead of looking for ways to compete with your personal best or looking for ways to cooperate so that everyone can win, you see the world of business as a battlefield.

Our expectations should extend beyond both a fear of poverty and an expectation of prosperity. A better and more realistic expectation is to trust in, and search for, sufficiency.

Self-identity, security, economic justice, and corporate social responsibility flow from your spirituality. Justice depends on your conviction that you belong in the universe. The wisdom of our society and of our evolutionary biological history says that we must take care of ourselves first. We think that after we take care of ourselves we can relax and take it easy. So we spend years climbing the ladder of success, thinking that then we will have earned the right to relax and live. Looking up from the bottom, we see the top of the ladder disappearing into a cloud of abundance and security—usually defined as money.

But often if we succeed in reaching the top of the ladder, we discover that we have no more security or satisfaction at the top than we had at the bottom. We have focused solely, or at least primarily, on ourselves and our own needs. Our goal has been on getting, having, and keeping. Think instead about physics: When we need heat or cooling, we want movement in the air to bring us the heat or cooling. When we want water to drink, we do not go to a stagnant pool. When we need the power of electricity, we must keep the circuits open.

In order to be in the flow of life itself, we must not keep and hoard anything of any kind for only ourselves. Instead, we must let goods and compliments and success and blessings and life itself *flow through* us. Anything that stops the flow of blessings, of goodness, of material goods, also stops the flow of life. It is a rule of life itself: life is maintained and furthered only when the channels of reciprocity are kept open.

For further reflection, it may be helpful to review the discussions of openness on page 54 and open behaviors on page 68, and the discussions of hospitality on page 55 and hospitable behaviors on page 69.

Making Connections

Are you connected? Janiece Webb, Senior Vice President for Motorola, says:

> If ever there's a time for spiritual leadership, it's now. You must earn the right to lead every day, and spirituality is necessary to do that. Spirituality means to be connected in a real way to life, with the center, at the core. How do you connect with people and stay together? How do you do that as a leader? Spiritual connection is the only way I know. You must connect with a person's soul, at the deepest core. You must

have your gut, head and heart lined up . . . not superficially engaged.[8]

We have discussed spiritual traits and behaviors at length in Chapters 5 and 6. Spiritual connection is related to all of these, but especially to compassion. Compassion is released and nurtured when a company and its managers and leaders understand that the workers—and other people among its stakeholders—are not just means to a business end, but are ends in themselves.

The following qualities relate to connectedness and compassion.

Servant Leadership

The concept of servant leadership is known in business because of the work of Robert K. Greenleaf, who spent much of his career at AT&T. After his retirement he wrote a series of essays and two books on servant leadership. Today the Greenleaf Center carries on his work in the principles and practices of servant leadership. The Center defines servant leadership as follows:

> Servant-Leadership is a practical philosophy which supports people who choose to serve first, and then lead as a way of expanding service to individuals and institutions. Servant-leaders may or may not hold formal leadership positions. Servant-leadership encourages collaboration, trust, foresight, listening, and the ethical use of power and empowerment.[9]

Meaningful Work

Compassion and servant leadership extend beyond the immediacy of the workplace to customers and suppliers. But within the workplace itself, what difference can your compassion and servant leadership make to those who work for and with you? In his column on work, Tim McGuire writes:

> If people are more important than machines, processes or excessive profits, then employers must make work well-organized, rewarding and just. Work that degrades people or disrespects them violates this principle and the managers or owners responsible can't claim they bring their spiritual selves to work. With few exceptions, every employee has special

things to contribute to the organization, but we often don't look hard enough for those special gifts.

Some people who pursue spirituality in their work are comfortable with an abstract approach to the subject. I contend decency must follow spiritual intent. Yellers and screamers, connivers and schemers and mean-spirited haters are going to struggle to find peace in the workplace, no matter how many silent prayers they utter. I know I did.[10]

Communication

Compassion, connectedness, and servant-leadership lead to real communication where the initiatives and the responses of employees are listened to and valued. The more you as a leader share honestly and seek the responses of the workers, the more you will build trust within the group and organization. Mary Ann Masarech explains:

Eliciting authentic response on a regular basis as a leader has a long-lasting benefit. The more you do it, the more the others will want to listen, and the more you reinforce your credibility— your trustworthiness, which helps you earn the right to be heard.[11]

Questions to reflect on include the following: Am I creating an atmosphere where everyone feels his or her concerns, ideas, and contributions matter? What questions or concerns can I anticipate? How can I stay attuned to the "question behind the question"? What kinds of individuals, attitudes, or situations make me feel defensive? How can I respond with generosity of spirit?[12]

Letting Go

It's not about you. The most common hindrance to the qualities of compassion, connectedness, and servant-leadership is the belief or feeling that everything—both process and outcome—depends on you. Sometimes all you need to do is be like a cup:

A Zen monk held up a cup and asked what was most important about it. One pupil said the handle, another the bowl, but the monk shook his head. "The most important thing about the cup," he said, "is the space it creates."[13]

Earlier (page 173) we discussed the relationship of power, authority, and responsibility, and said that whatever is delegated should also be consciously retained by the person higher up in the organization. This, of course, is based on the traditional hierarchical organization. Some businesses are changing the model. But even in an older hierarchical system, you can grow beyond the fear-based need to control that Parker Palmer labels "functional atheism," which believes

> that ultimate responsibility for everything rests with me. . . . An unconscious belief that leads to workaholic behavior, to burnout, to stressed and strained and broken relationships, to unhealthy priorities. . . . the unexamined conviction. . . that if anything decent is going to happen here, I am the one who needs to make it happen.[14]

Letting go of this fear is essential to becoming connected and compassionate and to developing as a servant leader.

For further reflection, it may be helpful to review the discussions of compassion on page 56 and compassionate behaviors on page 70, and the discussions of openness on page 54 and open behaviors on page 68.

Growing Your Courage

Is your courage big enough for your vision? In Chapter 7 we discussed vision at length. Living your life at work in terms of your spirituality, including both your vision of yourself as the person you want to become and your vision of your work organization, requires courage. Mary Ann Masarech explains:

> As a leader, you need to find your voice, to make the decision to actually lead from your personal convictions. Questions you might reflect on include the following: How important is it to me to speak out on this issue? Why am I hesitating to express my advocacy with candor (what am I afraid of)? What am I willing (or not willing) to risk in this situation?[15]

Your leadership and your ability to help others see your vision make a difference to others in your workplace. Masarech writes:

As a leader, you need to make the future "real" for those you are leading by painting a compelling picture. Helping people see more clearly what is ahead creates hope, possibility, and commitment. The more visual and vivid the description, the more compelling it is. . . . It's also necessary to describe the consequence of inaction. The human losses can include pride, morale, innovation, excellence, and community impact, among others.[16]

Leaders must lead. They are not merely coaches encouraging others but sitting on the sideline. Being committed to your vision requires courageous action:

Leaders go first. You, as the leader, need to publicly commit to what you will do regardless of others' actions. The more daring your actions, the greater the commitment others will be willing to make. . . . Once you have made this commitment, you have the right to ask others to act as well. . . . Questions to reflect on are the following: What am I willing to do regardless of what others may do? What specific actions will I ask the individuals on my team to take—immediately?[17]

Taking Risks

How do you rate on control, creativity, and risk-taking? Many business leaders micro-manage everyone for whom they are responsible. They are usually seen by their employees as controlling and difficult to work for. Perhaps you, too, are afraid of not getting approval or, even worse, afraid of public failure. This fear causes a would-be leader to maintain the status quo even when it isn't working and to continue committees and teams that are no longer productive.

Have you learned to take risks—even the risk of public failure? Are you trying to lead your group forward and make progress while also hating and dreading change?

Creativity is messy. You can see that especially in nature. The pollen in spring and the leaves in fall come down helter-skelter in an abundance that anticipates some failures, some waste, and a lot of cleaning up. You can't expect rigid order in a group that is stretching its thinking, fertilizing new ideas, and growing new products or implementations.

The creative process cannot be boxed in or tightly controlled. Creation comes out of chaos, and when that chaos is not tolerated, old procedures choke out dynamic creativity. The product and the process are dead or dying.

Are you afraid of the risks of creativity? Are you comfortable and secure only with rules and procedures for everything you and your group do?

It takes courage to overcome the urge to be too controlling and to tolerate the chaos that is essential to creativity. One way to calm your fears and develop courage is to learn and practice deep, centering meditation or contemplation, first at home. Eventually you will be able to practice it in brief moments at work also, thus restoring your peace and perspective.

Contemplation (sometimes called meditation or centering prayer) is a method of quieting and centering. Sometimes it results in a state of quiet that is inexpressible—beyond words. Thus, every description or definition of contemplation is expressed in poetry or metaphor: Here are four definitions:

> Looking deeply at life as it is in the very here and now
> — Thich Nhat Hanh

> The world becoming luminous from within as one plunges breathlessly into human activity
> — Pierre Teilhard de Chardin

> Seeing through exterior things, and seeing God in them
> — Thomas Merton

> Seeing God in everything and everything in God with completely extraordinary clearness and delicacy
> — Marie of the Incarnation

For further reflection, it may be helpful to review the suggestions for personal reflection on pages 58 and 72 and the Seven Developmental Tasks for Spiritual Growth on page 72.

Using Your Tools

What are your tools? If you are a carpenter, your level—sometimes called a spirit level—is the tool you use to ensure that your work is horizontally straight. A two-foot-long level is recommended for the most accurate results. You can also use the level to ensure that your work is vertically straight, or plumb.

Another tool you may use is the plumb bob. A plumb bob is made up of a string with a heavy balanced weight, or bob, on the end. You drop the bob from one point to find the next point that is directly below it, and mark the vertical line you need for your work.

What are the tools and criteria—the ethical and social justice principles—you use for making ethical decisions about your internal business and about the social responsibility of the company where you work? Is your level long enough? Do you drop your plumb line from a high enough point?

In other words, how extensive and inclusive is your own sense of ethics and social responsibility? Does your line of sight expand or are you wearing blinders, hoping not to see the implications and impact of yours and your company's decisions?

Facing ethical dilemmas is a difficult but rewarding, struggle. First you must identify which course of action is right. Then when you know what is required, you need the courage and commitment to implement the ethical action, especially in a situation of interpersonal conflict or potential business impact.

Are you courageous enough to be a whistle-blower if that is indicated in your workplace? If you are in management and someone in your reporting structure becomes a whistle-blower, how will you react?

For further reflection, it may be helpful to review the discussions of Vision, Values, and Ethical Principles on pages 78, 81 and 83.

Changing Cultural Values in the Workplace

On some positions, Cowardice asks the question, "Is it safe?"

Expediency asks the question, "Is it politic?"

And Vanity comes along and asks the question, "Is it popular?"

But Conscience asks the question, "Is it right?"

> And there comes a time when one must take a position that is
> neither safe, nor politic, nor popular, but he must do it because
> Conscience tells him it is right.[18]

Making a workplace spiritually friendly usually involves changing the workplace culture. The following sections discuss some of the aspects of the culture that need to be present to make the workplace truly inviting.

For further reflection in working on this task, it may be helpful to review the discussions of hospitality on page 55 and hospitable behaviors on page 69, and the discussions of gratitude on page 55 and grateful behaviors on page 69.

Valuing Spirituality

Your meaning, ethics, and passion are tied to your spirituality. If you park all that at the door when you enter work, you become less than human and little more than a machine. More and more employees are refusing to do that.

But if you as a worker are encouraged to express those aspects of who you are – and if your contributions are respected and valued by management and co-workers – then you can contribute to the overall good of the company and the work environment:

- Your morale improves because you don't have to compartmentalize yourself.

- When your morale improves, your productivity and efficiency improve.

- You can be less defensive. This frees up energy that has been spent in monitoring or defending yourself.

- When you are less defensive of yourself, you become more accepting of others and more cooperative with them.

- Having your spirituality affirmed helps you to integrate your left and right brain, integrating your analytical and artistic strengths and increasing your creativity.

- In business discussions around ethical issues, you feel free to share the spiritual basis for your own ethical beliefs.

Your role as a spiritual leader or manager is to encourage the spirituality of others and create a spiritually safe and friendly workplace.

Valuing Diversity

A spiritually friendly workplace must do more than value one particular type of spirituality. It must value diversity in general and religious diversity in particular. The United States Equal Employment Opportunity Commission provides guidelines for avoiding the following types of discrimination in employment:[19]

- Age
- Disability
- Equal Pay
- National Origin
- Pregnancy
- Race
- Religion
- Sex
- Sexual Harassment

But just as compliance with the law is not sufficient to define ethics for a spiritual workplace, so legal compliance with discrimination law also falls short in characterizing a spiritual workplace.

To create a spiritually friendly workplace, a company must truly *value* diversity, not just tolerate it. The Australian Government explains workplace diversity for its own employment policies as follows:

> Workplace diversity is about acknowledging differences and adapting work practices to create an inclusive environment in

which our diverse skills, perspectives and backgrounds are valued.

It is about understanding the individual differences in the people we work with that arise from our broad range of backgrounds and lifestyles, and recognising the value of using those different perspectives, ideas and ways of working to enhance the quality and outcomes of our work.

Our diversity is shaped and informed by a variety of characteristics including age, ethnicity, gender, disability, language, religious beliefs, life stages, education, career responsibilities, sexual orientation, personality and marital status.[20]

A spiritual workplace does not merely protect the legal religious rights of its employees. Rather, it values, encourages, and elicits ideas and opinions from employees based on their spiritual or religious values. This is a scary thing for many employers and managers to do. You do not need to allow proselytizing or criticism in order to invite employees to contribute their viewpoints and explain how those viewpoints have been formed and informed by their spirituality.

An essential element of workplace spirituality is the belief that leaders and managers have a fundamental responsibility to allow, encourage and motivate each worker to develop and grow to be the very best they can be. Growing individuals is as important as growing the business if you are going to find the spiritual in your work.[21]

Avoiding Religious Discrimination

David W. Miller[22] writes:

At the risk of offending several friends in the Faith at Work movement, I find it problematic when a company, particularly a publicly traded one, overtly embraces one faith tradition as its official or de facto religion of choice. Trying to make a company Christian (or Jewish or Muslim, for that matter) leads to several obstacles, not just legal but commercial and theological as well. Are we meant to build Christian companies, or are we meant to build great companies? Are we meant to be

Christian marketing representatives and Christian CEOs or are we meant to be excellent marketing reps and CEOs who happen to be Christians? In each case, I believe it is the latter.[23]

The legal risk of having an official religion is explained in Title VII of the U.S. Civil Rights Act of 1964, which prohibits religious discrimination by employers with 15 or more workers. Under Title VII, employers:

- May not treat employees or job applicants more or less favorably because of their religious beliefs.

- May not force employees to participate in a religious activity.

- Must reasonably accommodate employees' sincerely held religious beliefs or practices, unless doing so would impose an undue hardship on the employer. For example, employers might provide flexible scheduling or modify policies to accommodate an employee's beliefs.

- Are not required to accommodate employees' religious beliefs and practices if doing so would impose an undue hardship on the employers' legitimate business interests.

- Must permit employees to engage in religious expression if employees are permitted to engage in other personal expression at work, unless the religious expression would impose an undue hardship to the employer.

- Must take steps to prevent religious harassment of their employees.

It is also unlawful to retaliate against an individual for opposing employment practices that discriminate based on religion or for filing a discrimination charge, testifying, or participating in any way in an investigation, proceeding, or litigation under Title VII.[24]

Avoiding the Exploitational Spirit

Bob Fraser[25] distinguishes between the *entrepreneurial* spirit and the *exploitational* spirit:

I have had the privilege of rubbing shoulders with some of the best entrepreneurs in the world. Many people believe entrepreneurs are greed-motivated, but that is patently untrue. The most successful entrepreneurs are not driven by greed but by passion for finding and solving the greatest needs. When I teach classes on entrepreneurialism I am often asked how to find a great moneymaking idea. I put it like this: "Find the most people in the most pain, and solve their problem." The essence of the entrepreneurial spirit is meeting others' needs.

The opposite of the entrepreneurial spirit is the exploitational spirit which is more concerned with getting money from a customer (or congregation member) than providing value. People (or businesses, or churches) with the exploitational spirit pursue riches by using a customer to enrich themselves, instead of serving the customer. . . .

The exploitational spirit . . . sees business primarily as a means of cashing a check. Such people disrespect what I call the "sanctity of business" which is this:

Business is primarily about serving others, creating value, constantly improving products and services, committing to customers, being there for customers and supporting them long-term. It cannot be successful without intense passion and focus.

The exploitational spirit, on the other hand, tries to make as much money as possible and give as little as possible in return.[26]

In the current environment, sometimes a business exploits the workplace spirituality movement to get the workers more dedicated to the workplace, willing to work longer hours, and willing to give up time that might otherwise be spent in recreation, with family, in community or charitable work, or in religious practice. Some writers seem to suggest that because people spend so much more time at work, the workplace should attempt meet more of their spiritual needs.

If a company is based on noble principles, will its board and executives feel more self-righteous when layoffs come?

Is the workplace where people should be looking for spiritual fulfillment? Can business deliver?

Businesses should avoid trying to be all things to employees and simply allow individual spiritual expression, as long as that expression does not interfere with the rights of other workers.

Creating a Spiritually-Friendly Workplace

What happens if a manager decides to integrate more spiritual policies or beliefs or practices in the workplace, but his or her policies or beliefs conflict with that of other employees?

If a manager exerts subtle pressure on workers—even unintentionally—to endorse or share the manager's religious faith, then the company can be at risk legally.

But perhaps it is just as likely for an employee to face the opposite dilemma—one where management's practices appear to be in conflict with an employee's higher standard of ethics. Common areas of conflict are around issues of putting profit over quality, lying to customers, or polluting the environment. Or the conflict might be over giving lip-service to diversity and to a management style that is not supported at the top, or fostering competition instead of cooperation within the company. A worker may eventually have to decide whether staying there is detrimental to his or her own personal integrity.

Taking the First Steps

> Be patterns, be examples in every country, place, or nation that you visit, so that your bearing and life might communicate with all people. Then you'll happily walk across the earth to evoke that of God in everybody. So that you will be seen as a blessing in their eyes and you will receive a blessing from that of God within them.
>
> – George Fox

You can help to bring these changes to your workplace culture. As a spiritual leader or manager, you can:

1. Learn to truly value spiritual diversity yourself.

2. Post a calendar showing the religious festivals and holidays of all the faiths represented by your employees.

3. Accommodate differing spiritualities respectfully and establish a culture of zero tolerance for any action of religious or spiritual intolerance.

4. Allow workers to have a small spiritual or religious picture in their office, cubicle, or private workspace.

5. Allow employee-led faith-based groups for study, discussion, prayer, or other spiritual practice, during breaks or before or after work.

6. Set aside a meditation room similar to the kind of interfaith chapel you might find in a hospital or airport.

7. Accommodate religious dietary restrictions at company parties.

8. Educate other managers and supervisors in appropriate behavior relating to spirituality just as you would to appropriate behavior in other aspects of their supervisory role.

Questions for Reflection

1. Consider the traits and behaviors of the managers and workers described in Appendix C, "Troublesome Traits in Human Leaders" on page 217 in the light of the discussions of the "dark side" of leadership on pages 87 and 151.

2. What are some of the issues that affect each of these persons' ability to be a spiritual leader? What are the "shadows" in their personalities? What positive aspects of spirituality might help each person?

3. As part of your commitment to make your workplace more spiritually friendly, whether as an individual or a manager, consider the ethical pledge described in Appendix D on page 221.

Looking Ahead

In her book *Megatrends 2010: The Rise of Conscious Capital-ism*,[27] Patricia Aburdene identifies spirituality in business as one of the major social trends extending into the future. When asked in an interview for evidence that spirituality is a significant force in business today, Aburdene replied:

> First, the trend is developing in businesses all across the country, not just in certain geographic areas. Second, many employees have long been interested in the moral aspects of business, but when you see large numbers of CEOs getting interested in spirituality, you can be sure its influence is accelerating. [Third], you have a diversity [in approach].[28]

Three years ago Paul Wong wrote:

> The present spiritual movement is probably the most significant trend in management since the human-potential movement in the 50s. It appears to be a grassroots movement, as more and more people entertain the notion that work can be meaningful and fulfilling. In the wake of the Enron debacle, management is also more willing to take spiritual and moral values seriously.

> This trend [toward organizational transformation] will endure, simply because it speaks to the deeper needs of the human heart, and provides a promising remedy to declining job satisfaction. Even if research fails to establish a direct link between spirituality and profitability, an enlightened business attitude may still have the benefit of creating a more compassionate, caring and ethical workplace. This alone would be good news for people, who spend most of their adult lives at work.[29]

And so the movement continues. Our ideas about the purpose of business, expressions of new forms of capitalism, attention to business ethics and to corporate social responsibility, and the development of a spiritually friendly workplace are changing, growing, and developing.

And Next . . .

To order additional copies of this book for yourself or friends, please check with your local bookstore or favorite online bookseller, or visit www.AxialAgePublishing.com and place your order directly with the publisher.

I have written this book from a position of pluralism. Workplace Spirituality should be enriching for people of all faiths and all spiritualities.

Watch for my next book, which will be a smaller guidebook for Christian study groups to use *with* this book:

Workplace Spirituality: A Study Guide for Christian Discussion (for use with Workplace Spirituality: A Complete Guide for Business Leaders)
ISBN: 0-9778047-4-7

Other titles under consideration are:

Workplace Spirituality: Choosing Your Next Career

Workplace Spirituality: A Guide for Pastors

Workplace Spirituality: The Logical Evolution of a Movement

Endnotes

1 Father Richard Rohr, Founder of the Center for Action and Contemplation
http://www.cacradicalgrace.org/conferences/politics/politics_overview.html
(Accessed October 20, 2005)
2 Small Business Administration, "Leading vs. Managing—They're Two Different Animals" http://www.sba.gov/managing/leadership/leadvmanage.html
(Accessed August 31, 2005)
3 *Ibid.*
4 John P. Kotter, "What Leaders Really Do," Harvard Business Review, J. P.
(1990, May-June), Article Description, Harvard Business Online,
http://harvardbusinessonline.hbsp.harvard.edu/b02/en/common/item_
detail.jhtml?id=R0111F&referral=1043 (Accessed October 21, 2005)
5 Jonathan Wallace, "Leadership," *The Ethical Spectacle,* October 1998, p. 3,
http://www.spectacle.org (Accessed February 12, 2005)
6 *Ibid.*
7 *Ibid.*
8 Janiece Webb, Senior Vice President for Motorola. Spirit in Business,
http://72.14.203.104/search?q=cache:1cbHg-ZM_fcJ:
www.spiritinbusiness.org/quotes.php+Janiece+Webb+spirituality&hl=en
(Accessed December 3, 2005)
9 "What Is Servant Leadership," Greenleaf Center,
http://www.greenleaf.org/leadership/servant-leadership/What-is-Servant-
Leadership.html (Accessed January 1, 2005)
10 Tim McGuire, "More than Work" column for November 3, 2003, Copyright
2005, More than Work Distributed by United Feature Syndicate, Inc.
http://www.timjmcguire.com/columns_output.asp?columnID=5
(Accessed September 8, 2005)
11 Mary Ann Masarech, "AUTHENTIC LEADERSHIP: A CHALLENGE AND A
PROCESS," preprint of an article published in *Employment Relations Today,*
Autumn 2001, p. 5. http://www.blessingwhite.com/Library/Press/
AuthenticLeadership.pdf (Accessed August 29, 2005)
12 *Ibid.,* p. 6.
13 "Dreams Engineers Have" By Richard Thieme, *The Ethical Spectacle,*
http://www.spectacle.org/997/thieme.html, Accessed February 20, 2006
14 Parker J. Palmer, *Leading From Within: Reflections On spirituality And
Leadership,* an address to the Annual Celebration Dinner of the Indiana Office for Campus Ministries, 1990
15 *Ibid.,* p. 2-3.
16 *Ibid.,* p. 6.
17 *Ibid.,* p. 5.
18 Martin Luther King, Jr., in an address to Southern Christian Leadership Conference (SCLC) ministers
19 EEOC, http://www.eeoc.gov/ (Accessed January 3, 2005)
20 Department of Employment and Workplace Relations, Workplace Diversity
Strategy 2003-2005 http://www.dewrsb.gov.au/publications/_workplace
DiversityStrategy/default.asp (Accessed January 3, 2005)

21 Tim McGuire, "More than Work" column for November 3, 2003, Copyright 2005, More than Work Distributed by United Feature Syndicate, Inc. http://www.timjmcguire.com/columns_output.asp?columnID=5 (Accessed September 8, 2005)
22 David W. Miller serves as Executive Director of the Yale Center for Faith & Culture at Yale Divinity School, and is an Assistant Professor (Adjunct) of Business Ethics. David also leads the Center's "Ethics and Spirituality in the Workplace" program. The mission of the Center is "to promote the practice of faith in all spheres of life through theological research and leadership development." Miller is author of the forthcoming book *God at Work* (Oxford University Press, 2006)
23 David W. Miller, "Religion & Business: A Christian Perspective" http://www.ethix.org/body.php3?id=280 (Accessed September 8, 2005)
24 Summary of relevant points, U.S. Equal Employment Opportunity Commission http://www.eeoc.gov/types/religion.html (Accessed October 21, 2005)
25 Bob Fraser is the director of the Joseph Company. Prior to co-founding the Joseph Company with Mike Bickle, Bob founded NetSales, Inc., a back-office e-commerce provider that became the Kansas City metro area's fastest growing company during the late 1990's. In 2000, Bob was awarded the Midwest Region Ernst & Young Entrepreneur of the Year Award.
26 Bob Fraser, "What to Love about Money," http://www.icwm.net/articles_view.asp?articleid=6152&columnid= (Accessed January 14, 2005)
27 Hampton Roads Publishing Company, 2005
28 Jane Lampman, "Trend-watcher sees moral transformation of capitalism," *The Christian Science Monitor,* October 3, 2005 http://www.csmonitor.com/2005/1003/p13s01-wmgn.html (Accessed October 30, 2005)
29 Paul T. P. Wong, "Spirituality and Meaning at Work," September, 2003. http://www.meaning.ca/articles/presidents_column/spirituality_work_sept03.htm (Accessed September 1, 2005)

Part V Additional Resources

Appendixes A-D: Reference, Discussion, and Action

Appendix A Business Awards

This Appendix provides information about the following business awards. All the information is quoted from the websites indicated.

෨෨෨෨෨෨෨෨෨෨෨෨෨෨෨෨෨෨෨෨෨෨෨෨෨෨෨෨෨෨

Business Civic Leadership Center Corporate Citizenship Awards

Each year, the Business Civic Leadership Center (BCLC), an affiliate of the U.S. Chamber of Commerce, recognizes the achievements of extraordinary corporate citizenship in the United States and overseas where American businesses have an active presence. The awards showcase businesses, trade associations and chambers of commerce that have demonstrated ethical leadership and corporate stewardship, made a difference in their communities, and contributed to the advancement of important economic and social goals.

Five awards are presented:

- Citizenship in Action Award

  The Citizenship in Action award recognizes a specific action.

In 2005, a special tribute was paid to the hundreds of American companies that gave time, money, resources, and services to aid the response to the Dec. 26, 2004, tsunami in South Asia.

- Community Service Awards

The U.S. Community Service Award (given in 2005 to Xerox® Corporation) and the International Community Service Award (given in 2005 Alticor, Inc.) are presented to a business, trade association or chamber of commerce for a specific community service program promoting better corporate–community relations and contributing to the social and economic development of its community.

Companies and trade associations are eligible to compete for this award for the first time this year.

- Corporate Stewardship Awards

These awards (to small, midsize, and large businesses) are presented to companies that exemplify the highest ideals of corporate stewardship through their values, strategies, and operational practices. . . . Companies are recognized for their ability to integrate economic performance with a sustained contribution to economic, community, and social progress.[1]

Winners in 2005 were General Electric (large) and Citizens Financial Group (small/mid-size).[2]

Business Ethics Awards

Award winners should meet many (though not necessarily all) of the following criteria:

1. Be a leader in their field, out ahead of the pack, showing the way ethically.

2. Have programs or initiatives in social responsibility that demonstrate sincerity and ongoing vibrancy, and that reach deep into the company.

3. Have a significant presence on the national or world scene, so their ethical behavior sends a loud signal.

4. Be a stand-out in at least one area of social responsibility, though recipients need not be exemplary in all areas.

5. Have faced a recent challenge and overcome it with integrity, or taken other recent steps to show their commitment is currently active.

6. Be profitable in the most recent year, or show a strong history of healthy profitability.

7. For the Living Economy Award, be a company that is locally based, human scale, stakeholder-owned, democratically accountable, and life-serving, seeking fair profits rather than maximum profits.

8. For the Social Legacy Award, be a company that is focused on social mission which has successfully sustained that mission beyond the founding generation.

For details about these awards, see http://www.business-ethics.com/annual.htm#Criteria%20and%20Nomination%20Form.[3] To nominate your own company or another company, email Marjorie.Kelly@business-ethics.com.[4]

Business Ethics 100 Best Corporate Citizens

All companies that make up the Russell 1000 Index—the 100 largest publicly-traded companies in the United States—are automatically considered for the 100 Best Corporate Citizens.[5]

[To send updated information on your company, prepare a packet of information as described on the website, showing your performance and policies in the following areas.]

Social scores are done by KLD Research & Analytics in Boston. They rate each company in these areas:

1. Environment

2. Community relations

3. Employee relations

4. Diversity

5. Customer relations

For *Business Ethics'* rankings, we combine employee relations and diversity into a single measure of employee relations. What KLD looks at in each area will vary by company. There is no set formula. But the following gives some idea of the range of materials examined:

- **Environment** looks at positive programs in place such as pollution reduction, recycling, and energy-saving measures; as well as negative measures such as level of pollutants, EPA citations, fines, lawsuits, and other measures.

- **Community relations** looks at philanthropy, any foundation the company has, community service projects, educational outreach, scholarships, employee volunteerism, and so forth.

- **Employee relations** looks at wages relative to the industry, benefits paid, family-friendly policies, parental leave, team management, employee empowerment, and so forth.

- **Diversity** looks at percent of minorities and women among employees, managers, and board members; any EEOC complaints; diversity programs in place; lawsuits, and so forth.

- **Customer relations** might include quality management programs, quality awards won, customer satisfaction measures, lawsuits, and so forth.

For more information about these awards, see
http://www.business-ethics.com/annual.htm#Criteria%20and%20
Nomination%20Form[6]

Best Companies Lists from the Great Place to Work® Institute

Each year, the Great Place to Work® Institute produces various Best Companies lists in the U.S. including Fortune's "100 Best Companies to Work For"® in America.

We use the same selection methodology for the U.S. lists as for our over 20 international lists, including "Best Companies to Work for" lists in all 15 countries of the European Union, Brazil, Korea, and a number of other countries throughout Latin America and Asia.

Companies are selected for the Best Companies lists primarily on the basis of their employees' responses to the Great Place to Work® Trust Index®, a proprietary employee survey developed by the Great Place to Work® Institute.

Further information used for selection to the list is provided by completion of the Great Place to Work® Culture Audit©, a two part management questionnaire, also developed by the Great Place to Work® Institute.

We take pride in maintaining the highest level of integrity in our evaluation process. Great Place to Work® Institute and its media partners will only publicize information about companies that make the list and, in addition, only publicize positive aspects of each company.

For more information, see http://www.greatplacetowork.com/best/index.php[7]

The Trust Index®

The Great Place to Work Trust Index is an employee survey tool that measures the level of trust, pride, and camaraderie within your workplace. Employee responses to this instrument comprise the majority of an organization's score for all of our Best Companies lists. We make this instrument available to accepted applicants for any of our Best Companies lists during the employee survey portion of the application process.

For information and a sense of the nature of the survey, see http://www.greatplacetowork.com/best/trust-index.php[8]

The Culture Audit[©]

The Great Place to Work® Culture Audit© is a management questionnaire that we utilize to gain a better sense of the overall culture of the organization. We only make this instrument available to accepted applicants. However, the information that follows will provide you with a feel for the nature of the questionnaire.

There are two parts to this instrument. In Part I, we ask about items such as employee demographics (i.e. number of employees in the U.S., voluntary turnover, ethnic breakdowns, tenure, etc.). We also ask general information about the company (i.e. year founded, revenues), as well as about benefits and perks offered to employees (i.e. on-site fitness center, percentage insurance premium paid by company for employee, number of holiday days).

Part 2 . . . asks open-ended questions that give the members of the company an opportunity to share with us various aspects of their culture. The questions in Part 2 relate to the Great Place to Work® Model© which is the focus of this component of the evaluation.

For more information about this award, see http://www.greatplacetowork.com/best/culture-audit.php[9]

᪲᪲᪲᪲᪲᪲᪲᪲᪲᪲᪲᪲᪲᪲᪲᪲᪲᪲᪲᪲᪲᪲᪲᪲᪲᪲᪲᪲᪲᪲᪲᪲᪲᪲᪲᪲

The International Spirit at Work Award

The Award was inspired by the late visionary futurist Willis Harman, PhD (1919-1997). Four groups "co-own" and "co-organize" the Award: The Association for Spirit at Work; the Spirit in Business Institute; The World Business Academy and the European Bahá'í Business Forum.

The award is given to highly successful organizations that explicitly nurture spirituality among employees. In an age of high stress work environments and corporate greed these companies stand out for their concern for the spiritual well-being of their employees. But how can spirituality be "okay" in a corporate setting? What do these companies have in common? . . . .

- Many people confuse religion and spirituality . . . but they are not the same. Spirituality is a trait we all possess. Religion is a common way people express their spirituality. But some people are spiritual without being religious.

- The Committee defines spirituality as having two dimensions: vertical and horizontal.

- Spirituality has a "vertical" component—a desire to transcend the individual ego or personality self. This dimension is experienced as a conscious sense of profound connection to the Universe/God/Spirit.

- Spirituality has a "horizontal" component—a desire to be of service to other humans and the planet. In the horizontal we seek to make a difference through our actions.

- Spirituality in the workplace means that employees find nourishment for both the vertical and horizontal dimensions of their spirituality at work.[10]

What is Spirituality in the Context of the ISAW?[11]

The Selection Committee offers this starting point for consideration, with the recognition that each individual may have his/her own personal definition of the term "Spirituality."

- **The innate human attribute in spirituality**. All people bring this as an integral part of themselves to the workplace.

- **The "vertical" component in spirituality**—a desire to transcend the individual ego or personality self. The name you put on the vertical component might be God, Spirit, Universe, Higher Power or something else. There are a great many names for this vertical dimension. This dimension is experienced as a conscious sense of profound connection to the Universe/ God/Spirit. This might be experienced internally as moments of awe or peak experiences. A strong, sustained vertical component reflects in outer behaviors as a person (or group) who is centered and able to tap into deep inner strength and wisdom. Generally quiet time, time in nature, or other reflective activities or practices are required to access the "vertical" component of our spirituality.

- **The "horizontal" component in spirituality**—a desire to be of service to other humans and the planet. In the horizontal we seek to make a difference through our actions. This dimension is manifested externally. A person with a strong "vertical connection" who is also able to demonstrate the "horizontal dimension" has a clear grasp on his/her mission, ethics, values. A strong "horizontal" component is demonstrated by a service orientation, compassion, and a well-aligned vision/mission and values that are carried out in productive effective services and products.

- **Spirituality in the workplace** means that employees find nourishment for both the vertical and horizontal dimensions of their spirituality at work. Examples of vertical organizational spirituality include: meditation time at the beginning of meetings, retreat or spiritual training time set aside for employees, appropriate accommodation of employee prayer practices, and openly asking questions to test if company actions are aligned with higher meaning and purpose. Companies with a strong sense of the horizontal will generally demonstrate some or all of the following: caring behaviors among co-workers; a social responsibility orientation; strong service commitments to customers; environmental sensitivity; and a significant volume of community service activities. The vertical and horizontal dimensions should be well integrated—so that motivations (sourced from the vertical) and actions (horizontal manifestations) are explicitly linked. We will be honoring organizations that are financially sound (SUSTAINABLE) and effective, as well as focused on greater meaning and purpose. We believe that when done properly, Spirit at Work enhances the overall value of the organization.

The phrase *"Explicitly* spiritual" means that the topic of spirituality is openly discussed—not just assumed or implied. In the past some groups have called their initiatives Team Building or Leadership...yet what they really wanted was to create a more spiritual work environment. The drive to make a difference in the world for them was a spiritual hunger. Now they are willing to discuss this openly. These are the kinds of organizations we are seeking for the International Spirit at Work Award.

Endnotes

1   http://www.uschamber.com/bclc/awards/default (Accessed January 31, 2006)
2   For the 2006 criteria and nominations kit, see http://www.uschamber.com/NR/rdonlyres/eloxtt6bd7djzmr3uu464st3z2ormalotjkdfdk2hfy3x5v4xggs774icviofvso3uodabnembbmy5loketfaiylj3g/BCLCAwardsNominationKit2006.pdf (Accessed February 28, 2006)
3   (Accessed September 7, 2005)
4   Or mail to *Business Ethics*, 2845 Harriet Avenue, Suite 207, PO Box 8439, Minneapolis MN 55408. The Awards appear in the final issue each year. See http://www.business-ethics.com/annual.htm#Criteria%20and%20Nomination%20Form (Accessed September 7, 2005)
5   For more information, see http://www.business-ethics.com/whats_new/100best.html (Accessed September 7, 2005)
6   Accessed September 7, 2005
7   Accessed February 18, 2005
8   Accessed February 18, 2005
9   Accessed February 18, 2005
10 http://www.spiritatwork.org/awards/willisharman/background.html (Accessed September 7, 2005)
11 "Application for the 2006 International Spirit at Work Award," http://www.spiritatwork.org/awards/willisharman/docs/ISAWAPPLICATION2006.pdf (Accessed February 27, 2006)

Appendix B   Ethical Dilemmas in Today's Business

Many of the most highly respected companies and individuals are eventually the most highly criticized. This appendix contains six examples of corporate ethical dilemmas for your reflection. Considering Chapters 7-10 and 11, what advice would give each company if you were either a senior executive or a member of the Board?

As you reflect on these companies, consider their size. As of the end of 2004, Wal-Mart™ Stores, Inc. was the world's largest retailer. By the end of 2005, the final fiscal quarter alone of ExxonMobil™ would make it the 41st largest economy in the world. Its profit for 2005 (more than $36 billion) was the largest ever reported for any corporation and was "bigger than the economies of 125 of the 184 countries ranked by the World Bank."[1]

According to a study published in 2000, 51 of the world's 100 largest economies are corporations.[2] In an online interview, co-author Sarah Anderson observed:

> Right now, the rules set by the WTO, World Bank, IMF and other trade and investment agreements are designed to benefit large corporations. We need new rules that will put the goals of environmental sustainability, reduced inequality and human rights at the forefront. . . . we also need to get big money out of politics and to regain the spirit of monopoly-busting that has been subverted by the goal of global competitiveness. [3]

Enron and Kenneth Lay

Michael Novak[4] quotes Enron chairman and CEO Kenneth Lay as saying:

> I grew up the son of a Baptist minister. From this background, I was fully exposed to not only legal behavior but moral and ethical behavior and what that means from the standpoint of leading organizations and people. I was, and am, a strong believer that one of the most satisfying things in life is to create a highly moral and ethical environment in which every individual is allowed and encouraged to realize their God-given potential. There are few things more satisfying than to see individuals reach levels of performance that they would have thought was virtually impossible for themselves.[5]

Now under federal indictment for fraud and conspiracy, Lay's trial began in January, 2006.[6]

Wal-Mart™ Stores, Inc.

Wal-Mart has been ranked by *Fortune Magazine* as the world's largest corporation since 2002. In 2003, Wal-Mart ranked at the top of the survey of Most Admired companies. It is essential to know the criteria for any business award. This Most Admired award is based not on the opinions of customers, employees, or other stakeholders, but on the opinions of "10,000 executives, directors, and securities analysts" who rate companies in their own industries.[7]

Wal-Mart seems to be the store we love to hate but where we love to shop. The proliferation of articles, ethical and social justice analyses, lawsuits, and labor rulings relating to Wal-Mart has grown beyond a simple summary for this book. The battle and accusations continue. I encourage you to study the company for yourself; read both sides of the issue:

- "Is It Ethical to Shop at Wal-Mart?"[8]
- "Wal-Mart Fact Sheets"[9]

At the time of this writing, two movies about Wal-Mart are being released. Read "A Stepped-Up Assault on Wal-Mart" by Aaron Bernstein.[10] The movies are:

- *WAL-MART: The High Cost of Low Price*[11]

- *Why Wal-Mart Works: And Why That Makes Some People C-r-a-z-y*

    The documentary explores why Wal-Mart is one of the greatest success stories in business history, how it improves the lives of individual working Americans and their communities, and the social pathology behind the escalating attacks on the company by special interest groups.[12]

Tyson® Foods Inc.

Tyson® Foods Inc. is a company that is becoming known for its corporate chaplains. According to Jane Lampman, Tyson® Foods "has 127 part-time chaplains serving at 76 sites."[13]

The company's core values include striving "to be a faith-friendly company" and striving "to honor God and be respectful of each other, our customers, and other stakeholders."[14] It offers a free downloadable booklet, *Giving Thanks at Mealtime*, on its website "to help you discover (or rediscover) the joy and power of saying a word of thanks at mealtime."[15]

Tyson Foods Inc. received *Fortune Magazine's* award as Most Admired food production company in 2003.

Grandson of the founder of Tyson® Foods Inc., John H. Tyson became Chairman of the Board in 1998 and CEO in 2000. According to reporter Alex Johnson:

John Tyson has worked hard to clean up the company's image, tarnished by accusations involving illegal immigration and price manipulation and by some of his father's escapades, which culminated in the company's pleading guilty to a felony for giving gifts to Agriculture Secretary Mike Espy in 1997. . . .

Among his initiatives was to rewrite the company's statement of core values. An evangelical Christian, he worked with David W. Miller, executive director of Yale University's Center for Faith and Culture, to come up with a list of values studded with words like "trusted," "honorable" and "integrity."[16]

Tyson is on the Advisory Board for the Yale Center for Faith and Culture. Tyson® Foods Inc. and the Yale Center for Faith and Culture co-sponsored a national conference on "Workplace Chaplaincy: Hot Issues and Best Practices" at Yale Divinity School in August, 2005.

Johnson goes on to point out:

> Tyson Foods has made a lot of enemies over the years. Environmental activists scorn it for what they say is its pollution of the nation's waterways. Advocates for workers rights accuse it of running one of the most dangerous operations in the industry. Labor activists, especially, have taken it on as it drives down expenses in facilities it took over from IBP, where wages were generally higher than in the company's core Southern plants.

> Tyson has ready responses, pointing to awards it has won from the Environmental Protection Agency and citations for safety from regulators. It maintains that its wages and benefits, despite the cuts it has sought in numerous contracts, are the best in the industry.

> Tougher to answer are critics who question the chaplaincy program, suggesting that it exists mainly to put a friendly face on a union-busting polluter.[17]

In November 2005, the Supreme Court upheld the ruling of the Ninth U.S. Circuit Court of Appeals in favor of the workers at a Pasco, Washington, meatpacking plant owned by Tyson® Foods Inc.[18] The workers had argued that they should be paid for the time it takes them to walk to the production line from the area where they put on protective clothing.

Moreover,

> [According to OSHA] the rate of injury and illness at the [Pasco] facility is more than two and a half times the national average for meatpacking plants and more than twice that of meatpacking facilities with a thousand or more workers.

> The Pasco plant also stands out . . . [as] the battleground of a tumultuous effort to jettison the union . . . that has represented meatpacking workers there for more than 25 years.[19]

The complaints against multinational Tyson® Foods Inc. are extensive, especially in labor-related issues. On the other hand, Tyson gets both praise and criticism for its corporate chaplaincy programs. Religion has often played the role of keeping the marginalized submissive and accepting of—if not actually happy and grateful for—their lot in life. Does that mean that providing corporate chaplains is a bad thing?

John Tyson is said to be working hard to clean up the company's image and corporate behavior. Is it fair to expect immediate results? How does a leader or manager effect change in a large corporation?

ImmTher®, an Orphan Drug

Clinical trials for ImmTher, made by DOR BioPharma Corporation (formerly Endorex Corp.), began in 1999. The public became aware of the drug in August 2005 when CNN's Dr. Sanjay Gupta hosted a documentary on cancer. The program featured little Allie Krowski who was stricken with Ewing's Sarcoma, a rare form of cancer that is often fatal. Allie participated in a clinical trial of ImmTher which brought dramatic improvement within six months and apparently saved her life. At the time of the broadcast, Allie was almost six years old and still undergoing treatment, but DOR had decided not to make any more of the drug. When the current supply is gone, there would be no more.

In the broadcast, Dr. Eugenie Kleinerman, Chief of the Pediatric Division at the M.D. Anderson Cancer Center where Allie was receiving treatment said, "Sarcomas are a very rare tumor. And you have to understand that drug companies, pharmaceutical companies, have to report to their stockholders. And they're interested in their financials. And this will never be a money maker."[20]

I wrote to the company, asking why they developed a drug for Ewing's Sarcoma since I felt that they must have known—or should have known—that there were not enough patients to make the drug profitable. I challenged their ethics and corporate social responsibility, saying that they should have done "adequate market research and cost analysis before" they began. I concluded with:

> You have a moral and ethical responsibility to that little girl and to others like her to see that the drug is manufactured. That may lessen the profit to your stockholders, but it will hardly impoverish them or send you into bankruptcy!

A company representative politely responded, explaining:[21]

> . . . Because of the rarity of the disease, it was estimated that it would take at least 5 years to complete the Phase 2 clinical trials.
>
> With limited cash and personnel resources, the Endorex management team made the difficult decision in 2001 to cease development of ImmTher . . . . [and] took measures to identify a company with the experience and financial resources to develop ImmThur to its fullest potential, but the companies that were approached were unresponsive.

Then I learned that DOR is a small company with only nine full-time employees.[22] Its stock closed at an adjusted price in December 2004 of .64, and the price in mid-October 2005 had dropped to .28.[23]

Google™, Yahoo!® and Microsoft®

According to Reporters Without Borders (RSF), Google™ and Yahoo!® and Microsoft® have given in to China's government for the sake of commerce and profit. Microsoft is censoring specific words from its MSN Spaces blogging tool, including *democracy* and *Dalai Lama*. These and other banned words result in an error message that says, "This message contains a banned expression, please delete this expression."[24] The corporations either have not responded to RSF's request for comment or have excused themselves by saying that they are operating within the requirements of the individual countries where they do business.

Brad Adams of Human Rights Watch comments:

> There have been great claims by internet companies that it would be an unstoppable tool for free expression and the spread of democracy. But when companies like Yahoo!, Microsoft, and Google decide to put profits from their Chinese

operations over the free exchange of information, they are helping to kill that dream.[25]

On November 7, 2005, more than 25 socially responsible investment (SRI) funds and other organizations published a "Joint Investor Statement on Freedom of Expression and the Internet"[26] to promote human rights and insist that corporations not participate in suppressing dissent or free speech.

In April 2005 Chinese journalist Shi Tao was sentenced to 10 years in jail for "leaking state secrets" after Yahoo! in Hong Kong gave Chinese authorities information that they demanded.[27]

In January 2006,

> Google announced that it was switching its search facilities in China to servers based inside the country, and that as part of that process it would be cooperating with Chinese government censorship of the internet.
>
> Previously, Chinese users of Google had to access servers in America; the search results were then passed through Chinese government internet servers—"the great Firewall of China"—before getting back to the user; the Chinese government employs 30,000 policemen who work full-time monitoring the internet. . . Chinese net users who were blocked from accessing a site knew that the information was there and was being kept from them by their own government. From now on it is Google which will be keeping data from them, in direct contradiction of its own declared mission "to organise the world's information and make it universally accessible and useful".[28]

Endnotes

1 Dan Arnall, "Exxon Clears More Than 100 Million Daily," ABC News, http://abcnews.go.com/Business/story?id=1558860&ad=true (Accessed February 1, 2006)
2 Sarah Anderson and John Cavanagh, "Top 200: The Rise of Corporate Global Power," Institute for Policy Studies, December 4, 2000, http://www.ips-dc.org/downloads/Top_200.pdf (Accessed November 17, 2005)
3 Tamara Straus, "Study Finds Rise in Corporate Power," AlterNet, December 7, 2000, http://www.alternet.org/story/10184/ (Accessed November 17, 2005)

4   Novak is an author, teacher, theologian and diplomat.
5   Michael Novak, "Business as Calling," *American Enterprise*, July-August, 1997, http://www.findarticles.com/p/articles/mi_m2185/is_n4_v8/ai_19754358 (Accessed September 19, 2005)
6   "Enron's Ken Lay: I Was Fooled," CBS News 60 Minutes, March 13, 2005 http://www.cbsnews.com/stories/2005/03/11/60minutes/main679706.shtml (Accessed September 19, 2005)
7   Business Wire article on Find Articles, http://www.findarticles.com/p/articles/mi_m0EIN/is_2002_Feb_18/ai_83005550 (Accessed November 4, 2004)
8   "Is It Ethical to Shop at Wal-Mart?" Markkula Center for Applied Ethics, April, 2004, http://www.scu.edu/ethics/publications/ethicalperspectives/wal-mart.html (Accessed November 2, 2005)
9   "Wal-Mart Fact Sheets" http://www.walmartfacts.com/newsdesk/wal-mart-fact-sheets.aspx (Accessed November 2, 2005)
10 Aaron Bernstein, "A Stepped-Up Assault on Wal-Mart," Business Week Online, October 20, 2005 http://www.businessweek.com/bwdaily/dnflash/oct2005/nf20051020_3732_db016.htm (Accessed November 4, 2005)
11 http://www.walmartmovie.com/ (Accessed November 4, 2005)
12 "Why Wal-Mart Works: And Why That Makes Some People C-r-a-z-y'" http://www.galloway.tv/page15/page3/page3.html (Accessed November 4, 2005)
13 Jane Lampman, "Spiritual guidance... in the workplace?" *The Christian Science Monitor,* September 01, 2005, http://www.csmonitor.com/2005/0901/p12s03-lire.html (Accessed October 23, 2005)
14 http://www.tysonfoodsinc.com/CoreValues.aspx (Accessed November 17, 2005)
15 http://www.tysonfoodsinc.com/AboutTyson/TysonCares/GivingThanks/images/Tyson_Prayer.pdf (Accessed November 17, 2005)
16 Alex Johnson, "Walking the walk, on the assembly line" MSNBC, March 24, 2005, http://www.msnbc.msn.com/id/7231900/page/2/ (Accessed October 23, 2005)
17 *Ibid.*
18 "Meat-Processing Companies Lose U.S. Supreme Court Wage Fight," Bloomberg, http://www.bloomberg.com/apps/news?pid=10000103&sid=ayIeCJXb73EM&refer=us (Accessed November 17, 2005)
19 Sasha Lilley, "Meat Packer's Union on the Chopping Block," April 20, 2005, http://www.zmag.org/content/showarticle.cfm?SectionID=15&ItemID=7695 (Accessed June 20, 2005)
20 http://64.233.161.104/search?q=cache:-4RIsyiI_cYJ:ed.a.cnn.net/TRANSCRIPTS/0508/13/hcsg.01.html+Allie+krowski&hl=en (Broadcast August 13, 2005)
21 Personal email.
22 http://finance.yahoo.com/q/pr?s=DOR (Accessed October 22, 2005)
23 http://finance.yahoo.com/q/hp?s=DOR&a=11&b=2&c=2004&d=09&e=22&f=2005&g=m (Accessed October 22, 2005)
24 "Microsoft censors its blog tool," Reporters Without Borders, June 14, 2005, http://www.rsf.org/article.php3?id_article=14069 (Accessed November 17, 2005)

25 Daniel Howden "On the line: the internet's future" *The Independent* Online Edition, November 16, 2005, http://news.independent.co.uk/world/science technology/article327341.ece (Accessed November 17, 2005)

26 http://www.socialfunds.com/pdf/110805/Joint_Statement.pdf (Accessed November 17, 2005)

27 John Lanchester, "Big Google is watching you," *The Sunday Times Review* Jan 29, 2006, http://www.timesonline.co.uk/article/0,,2092-2014215,00.html (Accessed January 30, 2005)

28 *Ibid.*

Appendix C Troublesome Traits in Human Leaders

Referring to Chapters 5, 6, and 11, in each of the following examples, what are some of the issues that affect each of these persons' ability to be a spiritual leader? What are the "shadows" in their personalities? What aspects of spirituality might help each person?

Tisha

Tisha is a very intelligent and competent supervisor and project leader. She is great at projecting the length of time required to complete a project and she is affirming of those who report to her. She is also a good negotiator with other groups – as long as there is no overt conflict and no infringement on her "turf." Now there are issues of jealousy between Tisha and a colleague who used to report to her but is now her peer. The colleague suggested conflict resolution through one of the corporate human resource experts available to them. Tina refuses. She eventually explains that she does not trust people in the helping professions because of her experiences with them whenever she has advocated for her disabled child in the school system.

Mitsuya

Mitsuya is a bright manager with several people reporting directly to him. His direct reports are totally frustrated—it seems impossible to please Mitsuya. At each one-on-one meeting, the individual worker leaves convinced that he or she understands what Mitsuya wants. But at the next status meeting with him, Mitsuya inevitably says, "No, that isn't what I want," and gives a different set of instructions. For several months, each person reporting to Mitsuya thinks they are the only one with the problem. Finally, they compare experiences and his small group of direct reports is in tears.

Maria

Before everything was computerized, **Jorge's** secretary **Maria** kept the office supplies, including corporate forms that were occasionally needed by the group members. When a worker requested a form, Maria gave the person only one form. If the employee made a mistake on the form, he or she had to return to Maria and request another form. Maria's general attitude was one of being bothered by the interruption. She was not very friendly or sociable, and the workers perceived her as stingy. Since Maria's workday ended at 3:00 P.M., the workers would wait till she left to get the things they needed from the unlocked storage areas.

Barbara

Barbara is a recently-promoted, hard-driving middle manager in a software company. Though many workers are allowed to work from home one or two days a week and have proven themselves to be productive and effective, she insists that those who will be reporting to her give 40 hours of "face time" at the office. Barbara herself admits to having an unhappy homelife and has spoken of being eager for her children to turn 18 so they will leave home. She commutes two hours each way to work every day. The employees do not feel that Barbara understands or cares about their work/life issues. They also feel that she does not trust them nor respect their work even though they have proved their competence before her promotion.

Jeff

Jeff is a senior vice president. Like many top executives, he has "come up through the ranks." He wants very much to encourage and energize his employees. Senior management encourages the employees to play together in softball, soccer, etc., and many of them then socialize together at a local bar. In one impassioned speech, Jeff told the group of employees that he wants all of them – "your body, mind, and soul." Perhaps he is using hyperbole, but his comments make some of the employees wary.

Prabal

Prabal is a department manager who sees himself as empowering others. His stated way of operating is to communicate his vision to those who report to him and then leave them free to implement it. From the group members' perspective, however, that isn't the way he actually manages. He not only communicates the vision, but over time he also communicates the method of implementation that he expects them to follow. They feel that their creativity is not appreciated and that he promises empowerment but actually micro-manages them. His proposed methods do not always fit the style of the various workers and the result is often poor or mediocre results.

Appendix D Business Ethics Pledge

What else can you do as an individual to promote the ideals and concepts in this book?

"Take the Pledge" To Prevent the Next Enron

YOU are invited to help tell the world that:

- Businesses that run ethically, and understand marketing based on real human relationships, will be MORE profitable

- Profitability can be achieved regardless of market share

- Competitors, as well as customers, can become a business's "unpaid sales force"

Shel Horowitz, marketing consultant and author of *Principled Profit: Marketing That Puts People First*,[1] has initiated an effort to find 25,000 people who will "sign the pledge" and spread the message to at least 100 people. The pledge states:

> I pledge allegiance, in my heart and soul, to the concepts of honesty, integrity, and quality in business. I recognize that the cornerstone of success is treating all stakeholders fairly, with compassion, and with a commitment to service. Working from abundance, I recognize that even my competitors can become important allies. I will not tolerate crooked practices in my business, from co-workers, direct or indirect reports, supervisors, managers, suppliers, or anyone else—and if I encounter such practices, I will refuse to go along with them and report them to appropriate authorities within and outside the company. I pledge to support the "triple bottom line" of

environmental, social, and financial responsibility. And I pledge to participate in a serious effort to focus the business community on these principles, by sharing this message with at least 100 other business leaders.

- To learn more, see http://www.business-ethics-pledge.Org/

- To sign the pledge, go to http://www.principledprofit.com/ signethicspledge/index.php?sid=1

Endnotes

1 http://www.principledprofit.com/index.html (Accessed December 14, 2005) Horowitz' book *Principled Profit: Marketing That Puts People First* has won accolades from over 70 entrepreneurs, authors and marketing experts, among them Jack Canfield (Chicken Soup), Jay Conrad Levinson (Guerrilla Marketing), Anne Holland (Marketing Sherpa), former U.S. Secretary of Labor Robert B, Reich, and populist crusader Jim Hightower. It also received Honorable Mention in the DIY Awards, was a semifinalist in the Independent Publisher IPPY Awards, and was praised by the judge in the Writer's Digest Competition as a potential "breakthrough book."

Index

respect for, 177
spiritual nourishment of, 158
top seven goals for meaning and purpose at work, 39
Enron
analysis by Ed Konczal, 89
discrepancy between values and behavior at, 88
failure of, 87
values of chairman Kenneth Lay, 208
Entrepreneurial vs. exploitational spirit, 81, 186
Environment
relevance to investors, 111
Equal Employment Opportunity Commission (U.S.), 184
Erickson, Gary, founder of Clif Bar Inc., 86
Ernst & Young Entrepreneur of the Year Award 2000, 81
Ethical Corporation (EthicalCorp)
contests classic view of business, 99
Ethical dilemmas in business, 207
Ethical drift, 89
Ethical management
pitfalls of, 17
Ethical principles
in business, 83
Ethics
as expression of Workplace Spirituality, 38
code of, 84
companies recognized for, 85
cynical view of, 135
defined, 84
holistic approach to, 110
in business, 77
in Conscious Capitalism, 103
needed in leaders, 89
of a company, 78
public vs. business view of, 89
Ethics and Spirituality at Work (Pauchant), 17
Ethics and Spirituality in the Workplace program, 16

Ethics Pledge, 221
Ethics Resource Center, 87
European Baha'i Business Forum, 202
Evil done by people "doing their job", 53
Exercise for personal reflection, 43
Expansive solution
as a coping style, 37
Exploitational vs. entrepreneurial spirit, 81, 186
ExxonMobil
size of, 207

Faith
compared with spirituality, 10
defined, 2
embracing all traditions, 15
exploitation of, 10
in the workplace, 9
integrating with work demands, 15, 16
traditional, rejection of, 41
Faith at Work movement
David Miller on, 185
problems with, 185
vs. Workplace Spirituality, 18
Faith in the workplace. *See* Faith at Work movement
Faith-based workplace
vs. Workplace Spirituality, 36
Faith-free spirituality, 41
Fear
and illusion, 175
and need to control, 179
of, 39
of being imperfect, 175
of failure, 175
of public failure, 180
of scarcity, 39
of the creative process, 181
of unworthiness, 173
Findhorn Foundation
Consultancy Service (FFCS) described, 147
on fourth bottom line, 158

Printed in the United States
94440LV00003B/82/A

9 780977 804733